U.S. Fish and Wildlife Service

Waterfowl

Population Status, 2004

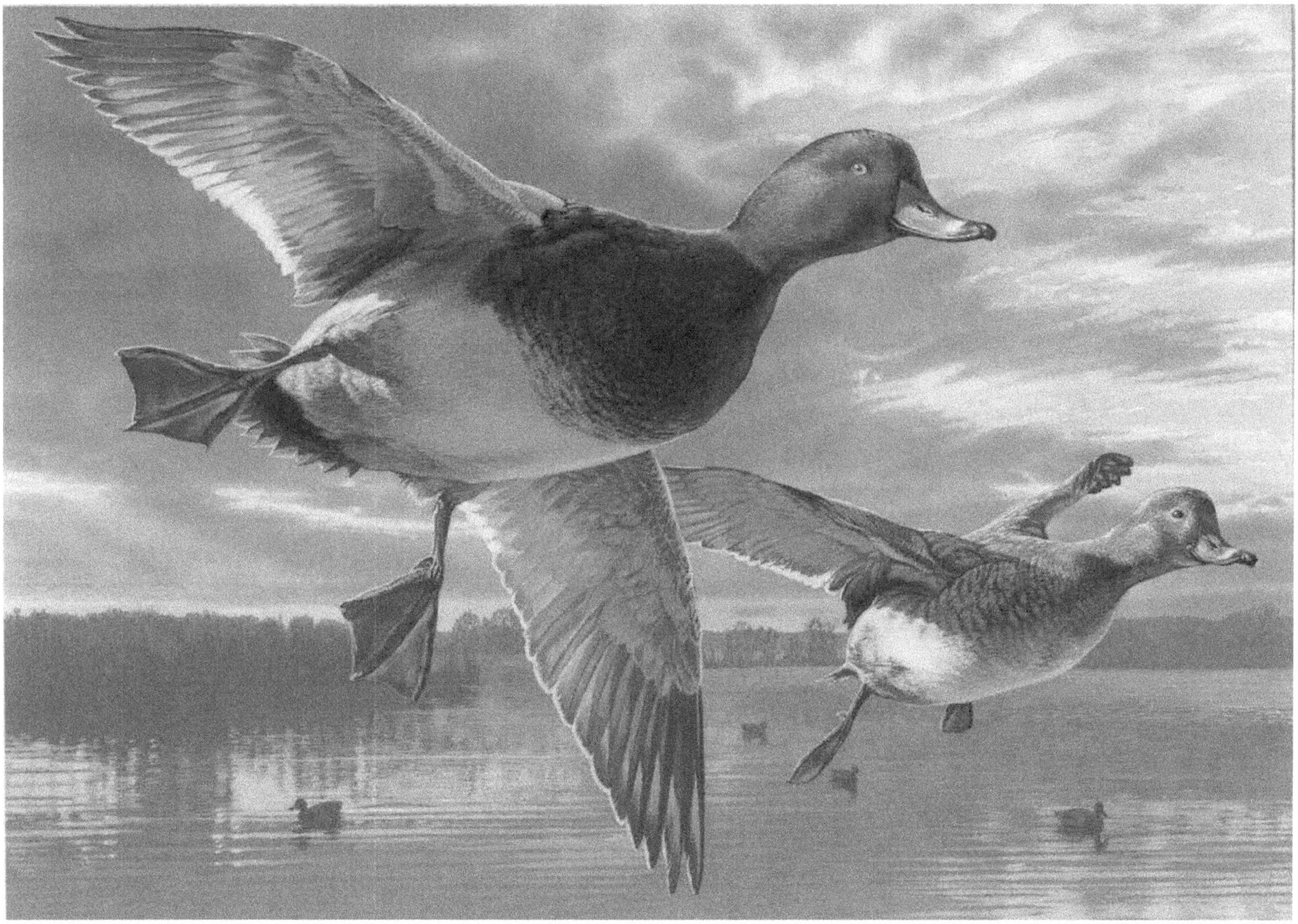

WATERFOWL POPULATION STATUS, 2004

July 22, 2004

In North America the process of establishing hunting regulations for waterfowl is conducted annually. In the United States the process involves a number of scheduled meetings in which information regarding the status of waterfowl is presented to individuals within the agencies responsible for setting hunting regulations. In addition the proposed regulations are published in the *Federal Register* to allow public comment. This report includes the most current breeding population and production information available for waterfowl in North America and is a result of cooperative efforts by the U.S. Fish and Wildlife Service (FWS), the Canadian Wildlife Service (CWS), various state and provincial conservation agencies, and private conservation organizations. This report is intended to aid the development of waterfowl harvest regulations in the United States for the 2004-2005 hunting season.

Cover art: Redheads. Scot Storm, winner of the 2004-2005 Federal Duck Stamp design competition.

ACKNOWLEDGMENTS

Waterfowl Population and Habitat Information: The information contained in this report is the result of the efforts of numerous individuals and organizations. Principal contributors include the Canadian Wildlife Service, U.S. Fish and Wildlife Service, state wildlife conservation agencies, provincial conservation agencies from Canada, and Direccion General de Conservacion Ecologica de los Recursos Naturales, Mexico. In addition, several conservation organizations, other state and federal agencies, universities, and private individuals provided information or cooperated in survey activities. Some habitat and weather information was taken from the NOAA/USDA Joint Agriculture Weather Facility (http://www.usda.gov/oce/waob/jawf/), Environment Canada (http://www1.tor.ec.gc.ca/ccrm/bulletin/), and Waterfowl Population Surveys reports (http://migratorybirds.fws.gov/reports/reports.html). Appendix A provides a list of individuals responsible for the collection and compilation of data for the Ducks section of this report. Appendix B provides a list of individuals who were primary contacts for information included in the Geese and Swans section. We apologize for any omission of individuals from these lists, and thank all participants for their contributions. Without this combined effort, a comprehensive assessment of waterfowl populations and habitat would not be possible.

Authors: This report was prepared by the U.S. Fish and Wildlife Service, Division of Migratory Bird Management, Branch of Surveys and Assessment. The principal authors are Pamela R. Garrettson, Timothy J. Moser, and Khristi Wilkins. The authors compiled information from the numerous sources to provide an assessment of the status of waterfowl populations.

Report Preparation: The preparation of this report involved substantial efforts on the part of many individuals. Support for the processing of data and publication was provided by Mark C. Otto, John Sauer and Judith P. Bladen. Ray Bentley, John Bidwell, Karen Bollinger, Elizabeth Buelna, Bruce Conant, Carl Ferguson, Rod King, Mark Koneff, Fred Roetker, John Solberg, Phil Thorpe, James Voelzer, and James Wortham provided habitat narratives, reviewed portions of the report that addressed major breeding areas, and provided helpful comments.

This report should be cited as: U.S. Fish and Wildlife Service. 2004. Waterfowl population status, 2004. U.S. Department of the Interior, Washington, D.C. U.S.A.

All Division of Migratory Bird Management reports are available at our home page (http://migratorybirds.fws.gov).

WATERFOWL POPULATION SURVEYS

50 Years & Still Counting

Next year is the 50th anniversary of the May Waterfowl Breeding Population and Habitat Survey.

Table of Contents

List of Duck Tables

List of Duck Figures

List of Goose and Swan Figures

STATUS OF DUCKS

Abstract. In the Breeding Population and Habitat Survey traditional survey area (strata 1-18, 20-50, and 75-77), the total-duck population estimate was 32.2 ± 0.6 (± 1 standard error) million birds, 11% below last year's estimate of 36.2 ± 0.7 million birds ($P<0.001$), and 3% below the 1955-2003 long-term average ($P=0.053$). Mallards (*Anas platyrhynchos*) numbered 7.4 ± 0.3 million, similar to last year's estimate of 7.9 ± 0.3 million birds ($P=0.177$) and to the long-term average ($P=0.762$). Blue-winged teal (*A. discors*) numbered 4.1 ± 0.2 million, 26% below last year's estimate of 5.5 ± 0.3 million ($P<0.001$) and 10% below the long-term average ($P=0.073$). Among other duck species, only northern shovelers (*A. clypeata*, 2.8 ± 0.2 million) and American wigeon (*A. americana*, 2.0 ± 0.1 million) differed significantly from (both 22% below, $P\leq0.003$) their 2003 estimates. As in 2003, gadwall (*A. strepera*, 2.6 ± 0.2 million, +56%), green-winged teal (*A. crecca*, 2.5 ± 0.1 million, +33%), and northern shovelers (+32%) were above their long-term averages. Northern pintails (*A. acuta*, 2.2 ± 0.2 million, -48%), scaup (*Aythya affinis* and *A. marila*, 3.8 ± 0.2 million, -27%), and American wigeon (-25%) were well below their long-term averages in 2004 ($P<0.001$). Total May ponds (Prairie Canada, and the north-central U.S. combined) were estimated at 3.9 ± 0.2 million, which is 24% lower than last year ($P<0.001$) and 19% below the long-term average ($P<0.001$). Pond numbers in both Canada (2.5 ± 0.1 million) and the U. S. (1.4 ± 0.1 million) were below 2003 estimates (-29% in Canada, and -16% in the U.S.; $P\leq0.033$), and pond numbers in Canada were 25% below the long-term average for this region ($P<0.001$). The projected mallard fall flight index was 9.4 ± 0.1 million birds, similar to the 2003 estimate of 10.3 ± 0.1 million ($P=0.467$). The eastern survey area is comprised of strata 51-56 and 62-69. The 2004 total-duck population estimate for this area was 3.9 ± 0.3 million birds. This estimate was similar to last year's estimate of 3.6 ± 0.3 million birds, and to the 1996-2003 average ($P\geq0.102$). Individual species estimates for this area were similar to 2003 estimates and to 1996-2003 averages, with the exception of American wigeon (0.1 ± 0.1 million) and goldeneyes (*Bucephala clangula* and *B. islandica*, 0.4 ± 0.1 million) which were 61% and 42% below their 1996-2003 averages ($P\leq0.052$), respectively, and ring-necked ducks (*Aythya collaris*, 0.7 ± 0.2 million), which increased 67% relative to their 2003 estimate ($P=0.095$).

This section summarizes the most recent information about the status of North American duck populations and their habitats in order to facilitate development of harvest regulations in the U.S. The annual status of these populations is monitored using a variety of databases, which include estimates of the size of breeding populations, production, and harvest. This report discusses population survey results. Harvest survey results are discussed in separate reports. The data and analyses were the most current available when this report was written. Future analyses may yield slightly different results as databases are updated and new analytical procedures become available.

METHODS

Breeding Population and Habitat Survey

Federal, provincial, and state agencies conduct surveys each spring to estimate the size of breeding populations and to evaluate the condition of the habitats. These surveys are conducted using fixed-wing aircraft and cover over 2.0 million square miles that encompass principal breeding areas of North America. The traditional survey area (strata 1-18, 20-50, and 75-77) comprises parts of Alaska, Canada, and the north-central U.S., and includes approximately 1.3 million square miles (Appendix C). The eastern survey area (strata 51-56 and 62-69) includes parts of Ontario, Quebec, Labrador, Newfoundland, Nova Scotia, Prince Edward Island, New Brunswick, New York, and Maine, covering an area of approximately 0.7 million square miles.

In Prairie Canada and the north-central U.S., estimates are corrected annually for visibility bias by conducting ground counts. In the northern portions of the traditional survey area and the eastern survey area, duck estimates are adjusted using visibility correction factors derived from a comparison of airplane and helicopter counts. For the 2004 eastern survey area, these correction factors were updated only in strata 68 and 69. Annual estimates of duck abundance are available since 1955 for the traditional survey area and for all strata in the eastern survey area since 1996, although portions of the eastern survey area have been surveyed since 1990. In the traditional survey area, estimates of pond abundance in Prairie Canada are available since 1961 and in the north-central U.S. since 1974. Several provinces and states also conduct breeding waterfowl surveys using various methods; some have survey designs that allow calculation of measures of precision for their estimates. Information about habitat conditions was supplied primarily by biologists working in the survey areas. However, much ancillary weather information was obtained from agricultural and weather internet sites (see references).

Production and Habitat Survey

In July, aerial observers usually assess summer habitat conditions and duck production in a portion of the traditional survey area (strata 20-49 and 75-77). This survey provides indices of duck brood and pond numbers. Ground counts are not conducted concurrently with July aerial surveys, so indices of duck broods and ponds are not corrected for visibility bias. The coefficients of variation for May pond estimates are used to estimate the precision of July pond counts.

This year, we had no traditional July Production Survey to verify the early predictions of our biologists in the field, due to severe budget constraints within the migratory bird program. However, the pilot-biologists responsible for several survey areas (southern Alberta, southern Saskatchewan, the Dakotas, and Montana) returned in early July for a brief flight over representative portions of their areas as a rough assessment of habitat changes since May and resultant duck production. This information, along with reports from local biologists in the field, helped us formulate our overall perspective on duck production this year.

Total Duck Species Composition

In the traditional survey area, our estimate of total ducks excludes scoters (*Melanitta* spp.), eiders (*Somateria* and *Polysticta* spp.), long-tailed ducks (*Clangula hyemalis*), mergansers (*Mergus* and *Lophodytes* spp.), and wood ducks (*Aix sponsa*), because the traditional survey area does not cover a large portion of their breeding range. However, scoters and mergansers breed throughout a large portion of the eastern survey area. Therefore, the total-duck species composition in the eastern survey area includes these species. Canvasbacks (*Aythya valisineria*), redheads (*A. americana*), and ruddy ducks (*Oxyura jamaicensis*) are excluded from the eastern total-duck estimate because these species rarely breed there. Wood ducks are also not included in the total-duck estimate for the eastern survey area, even though this species breeds over much of the region, as their wooded habitats make them difficult to detect from the air.

Mallard Fall-flight Index

The mallard fall-flight index is a prediction of the size of the fall population originating from the mid-continent region of North America. For management purposes, the mid-continent population is composed of mallards originating from the traditional survey area, as well as Michigan, Minnesota, and Wisconsin. The index is based on the mallard models used for Adaptive Harvest Management, and considers breeding population size, habitat conditions, adult summer survival, and projected fall age ratio (young/adult). The projected fall age ratio is predicted from a model that depicts how the age ratio varies with changes in spring population size and pond abundance. The fall-flight index represents a weighted average of the fall flights predicted by the four alternative models of mallard population dynamics used in Adaptive Harvest Management (U. S. Fish and Wildlife Service 2004).

RESULTS AND DISCUSSION

2003 in Review

Habitat conditions for breeding waterfowl greatly improved over 2002 in most of the prairie survey areas and those improved conditions were reflected in the numbers of ponds counted in 2003. The May pond estimate (U.S. Prairies and Prairie and Parkland Canada combined) of 5.2 ± 0.2 million was 91% higher than in 2002 ($P<0.001$), and 7% above the long-term average ($P=0.034$). Pond numbers in Canada (3.5 ± 0.2 million) and the U.S. (1.7 ± 0.1 million) were above 2002 estimates (+145% in Canada and +30% in the U.S.; $P<0.001$). Canadian ponds were similar to the 1961-2002 average ($P=0.297$), while ponds in the U.S. were 10% above the 1974-2002 average ($P=0.037$).

Most prairie areas had warm temperatures and abundant rain last spring. Two areas of dramatic improvement over the previous several years were south-central Alberta and southern Saskatchewan, where conditions went from poor to good after much needed precipitation alleviated several years of drought. Other areas in the prairies also improved over 2002, but to a lesser extent. However, years of drought in parts of the U.S. and Canadian prairies, combined with inten-sive agricultural practices, reduced the quality and quantity of residual nesting cover and over-water nesting sites in many regions in 2003, and limited production for both dabbling and diving ducks. Eastern South Dakota was the one area of the prairies where wetland habitat conditions were generally worse than in 2002, mostly due to low soil moisture, little winter precipitation and no significant rain in April. This region received several inches of rain in May, but by then most birds had flown to other regions with more favorable wetland conditions.

In the northern part of the traditional survey area, habitat was in generally good condition and most areas had normal water levels. The exception was northern Manitoba, where low water levels in small streams and beaver ponds resulted in overall breeding habitat conditions that were only fair. Warm spring temperatures arrived much earlier last year, in contrast with the exceptionally late spring of 2002. However, a cold snap in early May likely hurt early-nesting species such as mallards and northern pintails, particularly in the northern Northwest Territories.

Habitat conditions in the eastern survey area ranged from excellent to fair. In the southern and western part of this survey area, water and nesting cover were plentiful and temperatures were mild in 2003. Habitat quality decreased to the north, especially in northern and western Quebec, where many shallow marshes and bogs were either completely dry or reduced to mudflats. Beaver pond habitat was also noticeably less common than normal. To the east in Maine and most of the Atlantic provinces, conditions were excellent, with adequate water and vegetation, and warm spring temperatures.

In the traditional survey area, the total-duck population estimate (excluding scoters, eiders, long-tailed ducks, mergansers, and wood ducks) was 36.2 ± 0.7 million birds, 16% above ($P<0.001$) the 2002 estimate of 31.2 ± 0.5 million birds, and 9% above the 1955-2002 long-term average ($P<0.001$). In the eastern Dakotas, total duck numbers decreased by 21% relative to the previous year, but remained 25% above the long-term average ($P<0.001$). Counts in southern Alberta were unchanged from the previous year, and remained 38% below the long-term average ($P<0.001$). Total-duck estimates increased compared to 2002 in southern Manitoba, Montana and the western Dakotas, southern Saskatchewan, and Alaska ($P<0.012$) and were above long-term averages in the latter two regions ($P\leq0.001$). Counts in central and northern Alberta, northeast British Columbia and the Northwest Territories were similar to those of 2002, but 11% below the long-term average ($P=0.017$). Counts in northern Saskatchewan and Manitoba and western Ontario were down 21% from 2002 estimates ($P=0.003$), but unchanged

from the long-term average ($P=0.959$). The 2003 total-duck population estimate for the eastern survey area was 3.6 ± 0.3 million birds. That was 17% lower than the 2002 estimate (4.4 ± 0.3 million birds, $P=0.065$), and similar to the 1996-2002 average ($P=0.266$). In some other areas where surveys are conducted, measures of precision for estimates are provided (British Columbia, California, northeastern U.S., and Wisconsin). Total duck abundance was similar to the 2002 estimates and long-term averages in British Columbia and the northeastern U.S. ($P\geq0.171$). In California, the total duck estimate was up 36% relative to 2002 ($P=0.030$), and was similar to the long-term average ($P=0.177$). Of the states without measures of precision for total duck numbers, Nevada's estimate increased relative to 2002, but estimates for Michigan, Minnesota, Nebraska, and Washington all decreased compared to the previous year.

The number of broods in Prairie Canada and the north-central U.S. were 142% and 18% higher than 2002 estimates, respectively. Brood indices in Prairie Canada were 24% below the long-term average, while brood counts were 31% above the long-term average in the north-central U.S. The brood index in the Canadian boreal forest was 72% lower than that of 2002, and 76% below the long-term average. The late-nesting index was down 43% and 30% relative to 2002 in boreal Canada and Prairie Canada, respectively, but up 67% in the north-central U.S. Late nesting indices were below long-term averages by 74% in boreal Canada, by 43% in the north-central U.S., and by 46% in Prairie Canada.

2004 Breeding Habitat Conditions, Populations, and Production

Overall Habitat and Population Status

Most of the U.S. and Canadian prairies were much drier in May 2004 than in May 2003, which was reflected in the pond counts for this region. For the U.S. Prairies and Canadian Prairie and Parkland combined, the May pond estimate (Table 1, Figure 1) was 3.9 ± 0.2 million, which is 24% lower than last year's ($P<0.001$) and 19% below the long-term average ($P<0.001$). Pond numbers in both Canada (2.5 ± 0.1 million) and the U. S. (1.4 ± 0.1 million) were below 2003 estimates (-29% in Canada and -16% in the U.S.; $P\leq0.033$). The number of ponds in Canada was 25% below the long-term average ($P<0.001$).

Unfortunately, last year's good water conditions on the short-grass prairies of southern Alberta and Saskatchewan did not continue in 2004, and

7

Table 1. Estimated number (in thousands) of May ponds in portions of Prairie Canada and the northcentral U.S.

Survey Area	2003	2004	Change from 2003		LTA[a]	Change from LTA	
			%	P		%	P
Prairie Canada							
S. Aberta	888	511	-43	<0.001	726	-30	<0.001
S. Saskatchewan	2143	1461	-32	<0.001	1964	-26	<0.001
S. Manitoba	491	541	+10	0.280	674	-20	<0.001
Subtotal	3522	2513	-29	<0.001	3365	-25	<0.001
Northcentral U.S.							
Montana and western Dakotas	480	597	+25	0.018	521	+15	0.071
Eastern Dakotas	1188	810	-32	0.001	1006	-20	0.037
Subtotal	1668	1407	-16	0.033	1528	-8	0.243
Grand Total	5190	3920	-24	<0.001	4842	-19	<0.001

[a]Long-term average. Prairie Canada, 1961-2003; northcentral U.S. and Grand Total, 1974-2003.

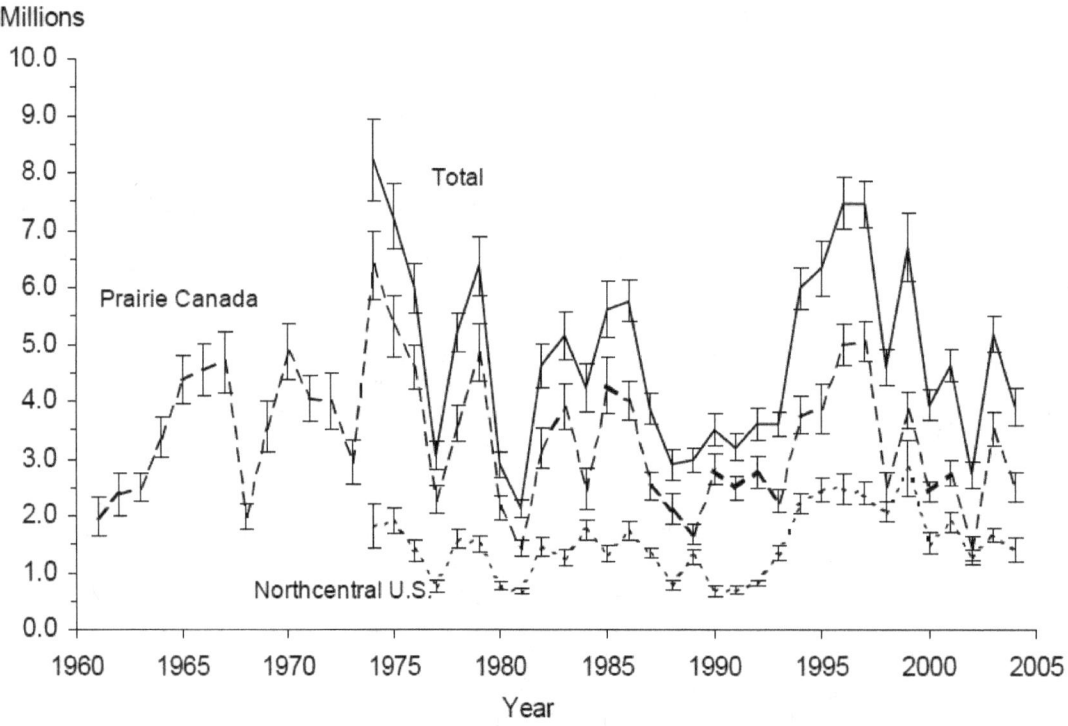

Figure 1. Number of ponds in May and 95% confidence intervals in Prairie Canada and the northcentral U.S.

habitat in these areas went from good last year to fair or poor this year. Habitat in southern Manitoba ranged from poor in the east to good in the west, conditions similar to last year's. In the Dakotas, a slow drying trend seen over the past few years continued, and much of eastern South Dakota was in poor condition. Conditions in the Dakotas improved to the north, and eastern Montana was a mosaic of poor to good conditions, with overall production potential rated only fair. Although prairie areas received considerable moisture from snow, including a late-spring snowstorm in southern regions, the snowmelt was absorbed by the parched ground. Furthermore, snow and cold during May probably adversely affected early nesters and young broods. Many prairie areas received abundant water after May surveys, but it likely did not alleviate dry conditions, because this precipitation also soaked into the ground. Therefore, overall expected production from the prairies was only poor to fair this year.

Spring thaw was exceptionally late this year in the Northwest Territories, northern Alberta, northern Saskatchewan, and northern Manitoba. This meant that birds that over-flew the prairies due to poor conditions encountered winter-like conditions in the bush, and nesting may have been curtailed. This is especially true for early-nesting species like mallards and northern pintails; late nesters should have better success. Overall, the bush regions were only fair to marginally good for production due to this late thaw. However, Alaska birds should produce well due to excellent habitat conditions there. Areas south of the Brooks Range experienced a widespread, record-setting early spring breakup, and flooding of nesting areas was minimal.

Breeding habitat conditions were generally good to excellent in the eastern U.S. and Canada. Although spring was late in most areas, it was thought nesting was not significantly affected because of abundant spring rain and mild temperatures. Production in the east was normal in Ontario and the Maritimes, and slightly below normal in Quebec.

In the traditional survey area, the total duck population estimate (excluding scoters, eiders, long-tailed ducks, mergansers, and wood ducks) was 32.2 ± 0.6 million birds, 11% below ($P<0.001$) last year's estimate of 36.2 ± 0.7 million birds, and 3% below the long-term (1955-2003) average ($P=0.053$; Table 2, Table 4, Appendix G). In the eastern Dakotas, total duck numbers were similar to last year's estimate ($P<0.590$), and remained 29% above the long-term average ($P<0.001$). Counts in southern Alberta were also similar to

last year's ($P<0.309$), and remained 42% below the long-term average ($P<0.001$). The total-duck estimate decreased 38% relative to last year in southern Saskatchewan ($P<0.001$) and was 22% below the long-term average ($P<0.001$). Counts in central and northern Alberta, northeast British Columbia and the Northwest Territories were similar to last year's ($P=0.160$) but below the long-term average ($P<0.001$, Table 2). Counts in the northern Saskatchewan--northern Manitoba--western Ontario area, and the Alaska--Yukon Territory--Old Crow Flats region were both similar to 2003 estimates ($P\geq0.106$), but above their long-term averages ($P\leq0.033$). Total duck counts in the southern Manitoba region and the western Dakotas--eastern Montana region were similar to 2003 estimates and to long-term averages ($P\geq0.354$). The 2004 total duck population estimate for the eastern survey area was 3.9 ± 0.3 million birds (Table 5). This estimate is similar to last year's (3.6 ± 0.3 million birds), and to the 1996-2003 average ($P\geq0.102$).

In British Columbia, California, northeastern U.S., Oregon, and Wisconsin., measures of precision for survey estimates are provided Total duck abundance decreased by 23% in California ($P=0.079$) relative to 2003, and was similar to 2003 in British Columbia, Wisconsin, Oregon, and the northeastern U.S. ($P\geq0.165$). The total duck estimate was down 31% in California ($P<0.001$) and 16% in Oregon ($P=0.042$) relative to the long-term average. In Wisconsin, total ducks were 58% above their long-term average ($P=0.001$). In British Columbia and the northeastern U.S., total duck estimates were similar to their long-term averages. Of the states without measures of precision for total duck numbers, estimates of total ducks increased in Nevada, Minnesota, and Michigan relative to 2003, but estimates decreased in Nebraska and Washington compared to last year.

Trends and annual breeding population estimates for 10 principal duck species from the traditional survey area are provided in Figure 2, Table 4, and Appendix F. Mallard abundance was 7.4 ± 0.3 million, which is statistically similar to last year's estimate of 7.9 ± 0.3 million ($P=0.177$), and to the long-term average ($P=0.762$, Tables 3 and 4). Mallard numbers dropped significantly in southern Saskatchewan and southern Manitoba compared to 2003 ($P\leq0.032$). Mallards were 23% below their long-term average in southern Saskatchewan ($P<0.001$), but unchanged from the long-term average in southern Manitoba. In the eastern Dakotas and Alaska--Yukon Territory--Old Crow Flats regions, mallard estimates were similar to those of 2003 ($P\geq0.726$), and remained well

Table 2. Total duck[a] breeding population estimates (in thousands).

| Region | 2003 | 2004 | Change from 2003 | | LTA[b] | Change from LTA | |
			%	P		%	P
Traditional Survey Area							
Alaska - Yukon Territory - Old Crow Flats	5705	5456	-4	0.361	3480	+57	<0.001
C. & N. Alberta - N.E. British Columbia - Northwest Territories	6461	5882	-9	0.160	7229	-19	<0.001
N. Saskatchewan - N. Manitoba - W. Ontario	3564	4085	+15	0.106	3554	+15	0.033
S. Alberta	2696	2499	-7	0.309	4342	-42	<0.001
S. Saskatchewan	9296	5783	-38	<0.001	7367	-22	<0.001
S. Manitoba	1582	1474	-7	0.354	1544	-5	0.393
Montana and Western Dakotas	1731	1615	-7	0.413	1620	0	0.955
Eastern Dakotas	5190	5370	+3	0.590	4169	+29	<0.001
Total	36225	32164	-11	<0.001	33304	-3	0.053
Eastern Survey Area	3635	3905	+7	0.534	3343	+17	0.102
Other Regions							
British Columbia [c]	8	6	-24	0.366	8	-18	0.277
California	534	413	-23	0.079	598	-31	<0.001
Northeastern U.S. [d]	1304	1418	+9	0.313	1400	+1	0.854
Oregon	298	301	+1	0.929	356	-16	0.042
Wisconsin	533	651	+22	0.165	412	+58	0.001

[a] Excludes eider, long-tailed duck, wood duck, scoter, and merganser in traditional survey area; excludes eider, long-tailed duck, wood duck, redhead, canvasback and ruddy duck in eastern survey area; species composition for other regions varies.
[b] Long-term average. Traditional survey area=1955-2003; eastern survey area=1996-2003; years for other regions vary (see Appendix E).
[c] Index to waterfowl use in prime waterfowl producing regions of the province.
[d] Includes all or portions of CT, DE, MD, MA, NH, NJ, NY, PA, RI, VT, and VA.
[e] Not estimable from current survey.

Table 3. Mallard breeding population estimates (in thousands).

Region	2003	2004	Change from 2003		LTA[b]	Change from LTA	
			%	P		%	P
Traditional Survey Area							
Alaska - Yukon Territory - Old Crow Flats	843	811	-4	0.726	341	+138	<0.001
C. & N. Alberta - N.E. British Columbia - Northwest Territories	852	776	-9	0.502	1103	-30	<0.001
N. Saskatchewan - N. Manitoba - W. Ontario	1103	1283	+16	0.417	1161	+11	0.482
S. Alberta	627	600	-4	0.766	1118	-46	<0.001
S. Saskatchewan	2111	1609	-24	0.011	2088	-23	<0.001
S. Manitoba	505	393	-22	0.032	376	+5	0.509
Montana and Western Dakotas	506	495	-2	0.891	502	-1	0.911
Eastern Dakotas	1402	1456	+4	0.727	823	+77	<0.001
Total	7950	7425	-7	0.177	7512	-1	0.762
Eastern Survey Area	383	368	-4	0.853	312	+18	0.358
Other Regions							
British Columbia[b]	1	1	+6	0.743	1	-27	0.015
California	337	262	-22	0.216	376	-30	0.003
Michigan	294	329	+12	0.614	436	-25	0.054
Minnesota	281	375	+34	0.158	289	+72	[d]
Northeastern U.S.[c]	732	809	+11	0.988	762	+6	0.993
Oregon	110	103	-6	0.563	130	-21	0.002
Wisconsin	261	229	-12	0.443	173	+32	0.050

[a] Long-term average. Traditional survey area=1955-2003; eastern survey area=1996-20013 years for other regions vary (see Appendix E).
[b] Index to waterfowl use in prime waterfowl producing regions of the province.
[c] Includes all or portions of CT, DE, MD, MA, NH, NJ, NY, PA, RI, VT, and VA.
[d] Value for test statistic was not available.

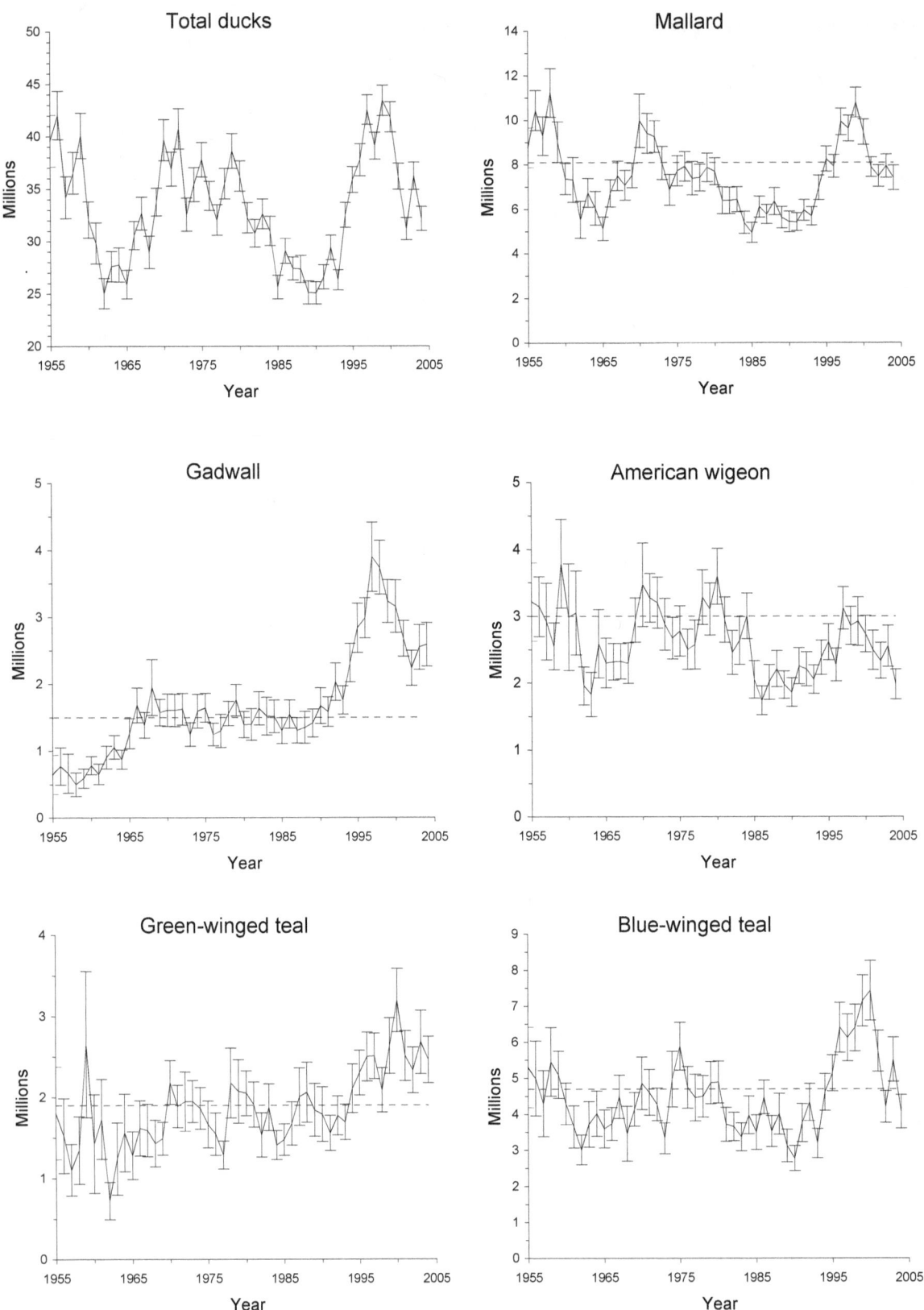

Figure 2. Breeding population estimates, 95% confidence intervals, and North American Waterfowl Management Plan population goal (dashed line) for selected species in the traditional survey area (strata 1-18, 20-50, 75-77).

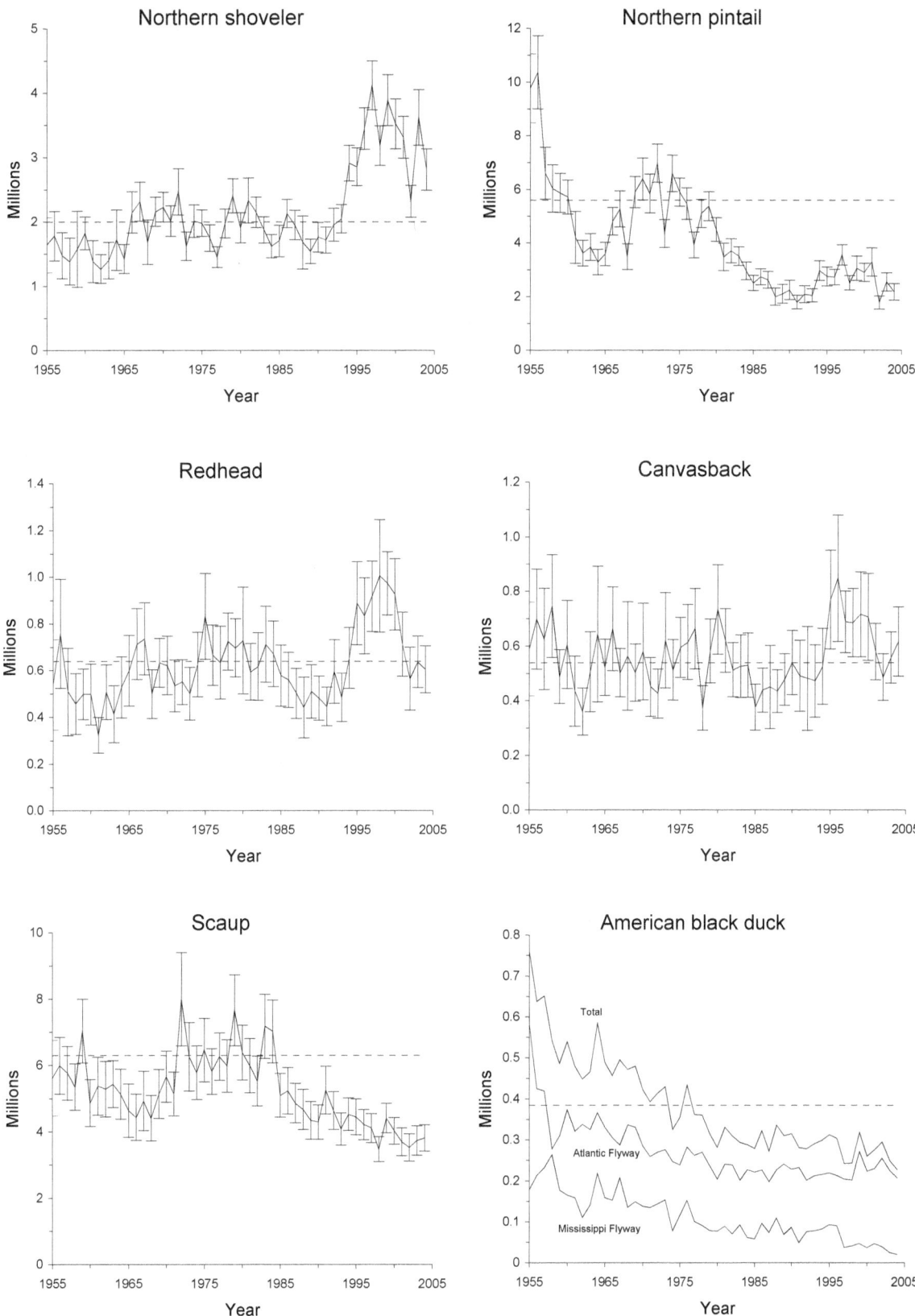

Figure 2 continued.

above long-term averages (P<0.001). Mallard estimates for the central and northern Alberta--northeastern British Columbia--Northwest Territories and the southern Alberta survey areas were also unchanged from 2003 estimates (P≥0.502) but remained below long-term averages (P<0.001). In the Montana--western Dakotas and the northern Saskatchewan--northern Manitoba--western Ontario survey areas mallard numbers did not change relative to last year's estimates and were similar to their long term averages (P≥0.502). In other areas where surveys are conducted and measures of precision for estimates are provided (the same states as for total ducks, as well as Michigan and Minnesota), mallard abundance remained unchanged from 2003. Mallard estimates were below the long-term average in Michigan (P=0.054), British Columbia (P=0.015), California (P=0.003), and Oregon (P=0.002), above it in Wisconsin (P=0.050), and similar to it in the northeastern U.S. (P=0.993). In Nebraska, Nevada and Washington, estimates of precision are unavailable, but mallard counts were down relative to last year's in Nebraska, increased in and Washington, and were unchanged in Nevada.

Blue-winged teal abundance was estimated at 4.1 ± 0.2 million birds, 26% below (P<0.001) last year's estimate of 5.5 ± 0.3 million, and 10% (P=0.073) below the 1955-2003 average. Evidence for overflight of the prairies by blue-winged teal was suggested by declines in population estimates relative to 2003 in all prairie survey areas except southern Alberta and Montana--western Dakotas, where numbers were similar to 2003 (P>0.384). Of the other duck species, only northern shovelers (2.8 ± 0.2 million) and American wigeon (2.0 ± 0.1 million) were different from (both 22% below, P<0.003) their 2003 estimates. As in 2003, gadwall (2.6 ± 0.2 million, +56%), green-winged teal (2.5 ± 0.1 million, +33%), and northern shovelers (+32%) were above their long-term averages (P<0.001). Northern pintails (2.2 ± 0.2 million, -48%) and scaup (3.8 ± 0.2 million, -27%) remained well below their long-term averages (P<0.001), in both total counts and in most individual survey regions. American wigeon were also below their overall long-term average in 2004 (-25%, P<0.001), and declined in all survey areas (P<0.001) except for Alaska, where they increased by 81% from 2003 (P<0.001), and the eastern Dakotas, where they were unchanged from 2003 (P=0.500).

Populations of most species in the eastern survey area were similar to last year's and 1996-2003 estimates. The ring-necked duck estimate increased 67% relative to 2003, to 0.7 ± 0.2 million birds (P=0.095). American wigeon (0.1 ± 0.1 million, -61%) and goldeneye (0.4 ± 0.1 million, -42%) were below their 1996-2003 averages (P≤0.052). All other species were similar to 2003 estimates and 1996-2003 averages.

The status of the American black duck (Anas rubripes) has been monitored primarily by midwinter surveys conducted in January in states of the Atlantic and Mississippi Flyways. The trend in the winter index for the total population is depicted in Figure 2. Midwinter counts of American black ducks declined relative to 2003 counts in both flyways. In both flyways combined, a total of 226,700 American black ducks were counted in midwinter inventories. This was 9% lower than the 2003 index (248,900), and 20% lower than the 10-year mean (279,800). In the Atlantic Flyway, the midwinter index of 206,400 was down 8% from 224,600 in 2003, and was 9% below the most recent 10-year mean (225,900). In the Mississippi Flyway, the American black duck mid-winter index decreased 17% from 24,300 in 2003 to 20,300, which is 62% below the 10-year mean (53,900). In the eastern survey area, the 2004 estimate for breeding American black ducks (730,000) was up 37% compared to last year but was statistically similar to the 2003 estimate (533,000) and the 1996-2003 average (498,000).

Trends in wood duck populations are monitored by the North American Breeding Bird Survey (BBS), a series of roadside routes surveyed during May and June each year. Wood ducks are encountered with low frequency along BBS routes, limiting the amount and quality of available information for analysis (Sauer and Droege 1990). However, the BBS provides the only long-term indices of this species' regional populations. Trend analysis suggests that wood duck numbers increased 4.3% per year over the long-term (1966-2003, P<0.001)) and 3.7% over the short-term (1980-2003, P=0.019). Specifically, in the Atlantic Flyway, the BBS indicates a 4.9% annual increase in wood ducks over the long-term (P<0.001) and a 4.2% annual increase over the short-term (P<0.001). In the Mississippi Flyway, the BBS indicates a 3.9% annual increase over the long-term (P<0.001), and a 3.5% annual increase over the short-term (P=0.009, J. Sauer, U. S. Geological Survey/Biological Resources Division, unpublished data).

Weather and habitat conditions during the summer months can influence waterfowl production. Good wetland conditions increase renesting effort and brood survival. In general, 2004 habitat conditions stabilized or improved over most of the traditional survey area between May and July. While there were no formal July surveys flown this year, experienced crew leaders

Table 4. Duck breeding population estimates (in thousands) for the 10 most abundant species in the traditional survey area.

Species	2003	2004	Change from 2003		LTA [a]	Change from LTA	
			%	P		%	P
Mallard	7950	7425	-7	0.177	7512	-1	0.762
Gadwall	2549	2590	+2	0.864	1664	+56	<0.001
American wigeon	2551	1981	-22	0.003	2637	-25	<0.001
Green-winged teal	2678	2461	-8	0.378	1849	+33	<0.001
Blue-winged teal	5518	4073	-26	<0.001	4508	-10	0.073
Northern shoveler	3620	2810	-22	0.003	2135	+32	<0.001
Northern pintail	2558	2185	-15	0.110	4182	-48	<0.001
Redhead	637	605	-5	0.681	625	-3	0.705
Canvasback	558	617	+11	0.458	562	+10	0.396
Scaup (greater and lesser combined)	3734	3807	+2	0.810	5249	-27	<0.001
Total [b]	36225	32164	-11	<0.001	33304	-3	0.053

[a] Long-term average (1955-2003).
[b] Includes species in table plus black duck, ring-necked duck, goldeneneyes, bufflehead, and ruddy duck. Excludes scoter, eider, long-tailed duck, merganser, and wood duck.

Table 5. Duck breeding population estimates (in thousands) for the 10 most abundant species for the eastern survey area.

Species	2003	2004	Change from 2003		Average [a]	Change from Average	
			%	P		%	P
Mergansers (common, red-breasted, & hooded)	569	668	+17	0.439	537	+24	0.264
Mallard	383	368	-4	0.853	312	+18	0.358
American black duck	533	730	+37	0.234	498	+47	0.137
American wigeon	79	27	-66	0.133	68	-61	0.004
Green-winged teal	452	554	+22	0.558	356	+56	0.123
Lesser scaup	101	81	-20	0.629	81	0	0.996
Ring-necked duck	399	668	+67	0.095	479	+39	0.225
Goldeneye (common & Barrow's)	768	430	-44	0.191	746	-42	0.052
Bufflehead	66	44	-34	0.260	60	-27	0.183
Scoters (surf, black, & white-winged)	237	261	+10	0.822	154	+70	0.200
Total [b]	3635	3905	+7	0.534	3343	+17	0.102

[a] Average from 1996-2003.
[b] Includes species in table plus gadwall, northern shoveler, northern pintail, eiders, and blue-winged teal. Excludes long-tailed duck, wood duck, redhead, canvasback, and ruddy duck.

in Montana and the western Dakotas, the eastern Dakotas, southern Alberta, and southern Saskatchewan returned to their May survey areas in early July to qualitatively assess habitat changes between May and July. Biologists from other survey areas communicated with local biologists to get their impressions of 2004 waterfowl production and monitored weather conditions. Habitat in some portions of the prairies, particularly in the Dakotas and Alberta, improved between May and July because of abundant summer rain. However, there were few birds in these areas because many had left the prairies in the early spring when habitat conditions were dry. Therefore, the production potential from most prairie areas ranged from poor to good and was generally worse than in 2003. Habitat conditions in the northern and eastern areas are more stable because of the deeper, more permanent water bodies there. Because temperatures were so cold in May, the outlook for production from these areas remains fair in the northern Prairie Provinces, and good to excellent in the eastern survey area.

Regional Habitat and Population Status

A description of habitat conditions, populations, and production for each for the major breeding areas follows. More detailed reports of specific regions are available in *Waterfowl Population Surveys* reports, located on the Division of Migratory Bird Management's home page. Some of the habitat information that follows was taken from these reports (http://migratorybirds.fws.gov/reports/reports.html).

Southern Alberta: The entire survey area recorded below-normal winter precipitation, with the exception of the Peace River and Cold River regions. In the spring, precipitation in southern Alberta was generally much below normal, except for Red Deer, which had fair conditions for nesting waterfowl. The prairie and aspen parklands (strata 26-29, 75) were in generally poor condition, with a few areas along the Milk River Ridge in fair condition. Stratum 76 ranged from poor to fair. The usually good habitat within a 50-mile radius of Edmonton was rated only fair this year. Overall, large groups of ducks tended to congregate on what little water was available. May ponds were down 43% relative to 2003 ($P<0.001$), and were 30% below the long-term average ($P<0.001$). Neither total ducks nor any of the individual species surveyed differed from 2003 estimates, but total ducks (-42%), mallards (-46%), American

wigeon (-62%), green-winged teal (−50%), blue-winged teal (-41%), northern pintail (-78%), and scaup (-66%) all remained well below long-term averages ($P<0.001$). Estimates of total ducks, as well as mallards, American wigeon, green-winged teal, blue-winged teal, and northern pintails were all at very low levels, ranking in the bottom 10% of estimates since 1955. Redheads were also below their long-tem average (-33%, $P=0.065$) Gadwall, Northern shoveler, and canvasback numbers were similar to long-term averages.

Habitat conditions improved slightly for production since May in western and central portions of the Alberta Prairies (strata 28-29) and the Aspen Parklands (strata 26-27). Most areas of southern Alberta received 85-115% of normal precipitation since May 2004, but continued above-normal precipitation is needed to restore water storage in wetlands to normal levels. Eastern portions of strata 26-29 remained in the poor category for production potential, and western areas were rated fair, with a few good areas. Palmer drought indices suggest that stratum 75 was largely in fair condition, and stratum 76 was in poor condition as of July.

Southern Saskatchewan: Waterfowl breeding habitat conditions across southern Saskatchewan were generally much poorer than they were last season. Despite normal or above-normal precipitation over much of the survey area (Strata 30-35), above normal fall and winter temperatures resulted in a poor frost seal, and most of this moisture was absorbed into the ground. Very little water remained on the surface for use by migrating waterfowl. The long-term drought in this region has taken a toll on the grasslands, and much upland nesting cover was in poor condition during the survey. The only bright spot was an area of south-central Saskatchewan in the grasslands (strata 32-33), especially important to northern pintails, that had good water.

The May pond estimate was down 32% from last year's count ($P<0.001$), and was 26% below the long-term average ($P<0.001$). Except for scaup, which were unchanged from their 2003 estimate, all other species in the region were down relative to their 2003 estimates. American wigeon were at their lowest levels since 1955. Population estimates of many duck species were below long-term averages (LTAs) as well. Total ducks (-38% from 2003, -22% from LTA), mallards (-24% from 2003, -23% LTA), American wigeon (-41%, -70% from LTA), green-winged teal (-54%

from 2003, -46% from LTA), redheads (-52% from 2003, -31% from LTA), canvasbacks (-38% from 2003, -34% from LTA), and northern pintails (-52% from 2003, -62% from LTA) were lower than 2003 estimates ($P \leq 0.022$) and long-term averages ($P \leq 0.026$). Gadwall were 30% below their 2003 numbers ($P=0.071$), but remained 37% above their long-term average ($P=0.094$). Blue-winged teal and northern shovelers were 40% and 45% below last year's estimates, respectively ($P \geq 0.022$), but similar to their long-term averages ($P \geq 0.166$). Scaup were 56% below their long-term average ($P<0.001$), but unchanged from their 2003 estimate ($P=0.240$).

The northeast Parklands region (stratum 31) improved since the May survey. Upland habitat was in good condition and most of this area had good-excellent wetland conditions, which boded well for re-nesting, late nesting and brood rearing by waterfowl. The northwest portion of the Parklands also improved, but has suffered an extended drought, and will require much additional precipitation to restore upland cover and wetland habitat to normal. Upland cover was rated fair-good, and water levels were good in existing wetlands. Overall, recruitment potential was poor in the southern portion of stratum 31, and fair in the north. Grassland regions (strata 32-33) were the most improved, but July conditions were variable. West-central portions remained dry, but in the few portions that had received moisture, conditions were good in this very important waterfowl nesting area. The south-central grasslands between Regina and Moose Jaw were very wet, with widespread flooding. While overall conditions have improved, biologists were reluctant to upgrade production predictions for the survey area. Many ducks had left the area by mid-May, and the cool, wet weather could reduce the survival of broods that were produced. The area was still rated fair to good for recruitment as of July.

Southern Manitoba: A late spring snowstorm in the central portion of the southern Manitoba survey area (strata 36-40) caused early-nesting species to abandon nests, but improved wetland conditions from fair to good. Additional rain produced many temporary wetlands as well as flooding, but biologists thought that few additional birds moved into the area as a result. The parkland habitat of west-central Manitoba was rated good, with good numbers of dabbling and diving ducks present. Overall, conditions for renesting birds and late-

nesting species were good. May pond counts were unchanged from the 2003 estimate ($P=0.280$) but remained 20% below the long-term average ($P<0.001$). Total ducks, northern shovelers, redheads, and canvasbacks were similar to their 2003 estimates and long-term averages ($P \geq 0.129$). Mallards were 22% below their 2003 estimate ($P=0.032$), but similar to their long-term average ($P=0.509$). Northern pintail and scaup estimates were similar to those of 2003 ($P \geq 0.176$), but remained 65% and 77% below long-term averages, respectively ($P<0.001$). The gadwall estimate was the highest since 1955 and was 57% higher than last year's ($P=0.075$), and 131% above the long-term average ($P=0.002$). American wigeon were at their lowest level since 1955 and was -78% below 2003 and 95% below the long term average ($P \leq 0.023$). Green-winged teal (-44%, -48% LTA), and blue-winged teal (-33%, -27% LTA) were also below 2003 estimates ($P \leq 0.032$) and long-term averages ($P<0.001$).

In late May, the survey area received much precipitation. Thus, although June precipitation was 50% of average, and July precipitation was average, as of July, water conditions in the southern portions of the province, along the U.S. border and near Whitewater Lake, were excellent, and the pothole country near Minnedosa was rated good-very good. Despite the apparently good production conditions, few broods were seen early on. Temperatures in late May and early June were well below average, and coupled with May precipitation, the cold may have reduced brood survival of early nesting species such as mallards and pintails. Observers did report more brood sightings in July, and the good water conditions improved the quality of upland cover.

Montana and Western Dakotas: In Montana (strata 41-42) and the western Dakotas (strata 43-44), waterfowl production potential was rated fair, and expected to be below average. In western South Dakota, water conditions had deteriorated relative to 2003 and many streams and wetlands were dry. By contrast, there was abundant residual nesting cover that likely benefited early-nesting species such as mallards and northern pintails. Water conditions in western North Dakota were better, but apparent reductions of land enrolled in the Conservation Reserve Program between Bismarck and Dickinson meant that good upland nesting cover was scarce there. In eastern Montana, wetland conditions north of the Missouri River were much better than to the south, and habitat conditions were rated fair to marginally good. The region south of the Missouri River was plagued by continued drought, and projected production was rated poor. Overall, May pond counts in the entire survey area were up 25% relative to 2003 (*P*=0.018), and slightly (15%) higher than the long-term average (*P*=0.071). This surprising rise in pond counts was due in part to drought-induced segmentation of semi-dry rivers. Total ducks and all individual species were similar to their 2003 estimates (*P*≥0.101). American wigeon (-41%), northern pintails (-52%), and scaup (-50%) all remained well below their long-term averages (*P*≤0.009). Green-winged teal were at their highest recorded levels since 1955, and were 177% above their long-term average for the survey area (*P*<0.001).

Overall, habitat conditions in the area stabilized or improved following May surveys. Brood rearing conditions were good, and production should be average along the Canadian border in eastern Montana (stratum 41). In western South Dakota (stratum 44) conditions were marginally good to the northwest, but only fair to the southeast, with mid-late nesters benefiting most from improved habitat. In most portions of western North Dakota, conditions were fair, with reduced pond numbers and water levels. The extreme northwestern tip of North Dakota was good for production, but overall brood production in stratum 43 will be below average. In eastern Montana south of the Missouri River (stratum 42), late rains produced lush green grass, which should produce good residual nesting cover for 2005, but will benefit only the latest nesters in 2004. Production will likely be below normal in stratum 42. Overall production potential for the survey area was below average as of July.

Eastern Dakotas: As a result of a dry and relatively mild winter, much of the breeding waterfowl habitat in eastern South Dakota (Strata 48 and 49) was considered poor. Temporary and seasonal wetlands were absent, and many had been tilled. Many artificial wetlands and small streams were dry as well. Wetland conditions in the Prairie Coteau were slightly better, and this area was classified as fair. In North Dakota (strata 45-47), wetland conditions were generally better. In much of northern North Dakota good breeding habitat, including seasonal and some temporary ponds, was present, and nesting cover was adequate or good. The remainder of eastern North Dakota was rated fair. Both states received considerable rain in mid-late May, but this likely arrived too late to benefit early nesters, especially in South Dakota. Later-nesting species and re-nesting females may have benefited from this late precipitation,

especially in North Dakota. May ponds were 32% below last year's figure (*P*=0.001), and 20% below the long-term average (*P*=0.037). Estimates of total ducks, mallards, gadwall, and scaup were similar to those of 2003, but remained 29%, 77%, 117%, and 169% above long-term averages respectively (*P*≥0.002). Blue-winged teal counts were down 23% relative to 2003 (*P*=0.062), but were similar to the long-term mean (*P*=0.984). Northern pintail numbers were 92% higher than in 2003 (*P*=0.020), but were 47% below their long-term average (*P*<0.001). The green-winged teal estimate was 159% higher than in 2003 (*P*=0.019), and 76% higher than the long-term average (*P*=0.059). Canvasbacks were 93% above their 2003 estimate (*P*=0.059), but similar to their long-term average (*P*=0.230). American wigeon, northern shovelers, and redheads were similar to their 2003 estimates and their long-term averages (P≥0.133).

Weather throughout the crew area from May to July was generally cooler and wetter than normal. This pattern improved water levels and in some areas, created "new" wetlands. The cool moist weather helped the development of upland cover, which was rated good or excellent as of July. Over-water vegetation was also very good, provided wetland basins were not recessed. Habitat in southern South Dakota largely improved from poor to marginally fair for production. Wetlands in extreme southeast South Dakota, the Leola Hills, the Prairie Coteau, and the northern third of the drift plain maintained their fair status and in some cases were marginally good for production, an improvement over what had been shaping up to be a near failure for production in the state. North Dakota also benefited from the cool, wet weather, but wetland conditions were better there to begin with. Wetland conditions as of July were good or very good in most of the state, yet waterfowl occupancy appeared low, especially on the drift plain. Response by late-nesting and re-nesting birds to the late water will likely be most pronounced in stratum 45, but brood-rearing conditions are generally good throughout North Dakota as of July. Moisture gains, if maintained through the fall and winter, portend good production conditions in this survey area in 2005.

Northern Saskatchewan, Northern Manitoba, and Western Ontario: In northern Saskatchewan and Manitoba (strata 21-25), habitat conditions for breeding waterfowl were fair to good. Most of northern Manitoba was rated fair, and the western edge of Manitoba and most of northern Saskatchewan was in good condition. Conditions in western Ontario (stratum 50) were rated good. In the extreme southwestern portion of the study area, near Big River, Saskatchewan, the timing of the spring thaw was near normal, but was very late in the remainder of northern Manitoba and northern Saskatchewan. Nesting conditions in northern Manitoba were also sub-optimal due to low water levels in many streams and beaver ponds. In western Ontario, spring was late, but water levels were high, with abundant rainfall in late May. Here, nesting was not expected to be significantly affected by late phenology. The late spring may actually have improved brood survival, as most females were still incubating eggs during the period of heavy rain, rather than tending newly hatched broods, which are particularly vulnerable to cold, wet weather.

Overall, the total-duck and green-winged teal estimates for the region were similar to those of 2003 ($P\geq0.160$), but were 15% ($P=0.033$) and 96% ($P<0.001$) above their long-term averages. American wigeon and northern pintails were also similar to their 2003 estimates ($P\geq0.236$), but were 42% and 76% below their long-term averages, respectively ($P<0.001$). Blue-winged teal were 67% below their 2003 estimate, and 78% below their long-term average ($P\leq0.006$). Canvasbacks, scaup, and northern shovelers were 277%, 64%, and 226% above their 2003 estimates, respectively ($P\leq0.011$), but similar to their long-term averages ($P\geq0.219$). Mallard, gadwall and redhead estimates were similar to those of 2003 and their long-term averages ($P\geq0.417$). As of July, northern Saskatchewan was rated average for production and northern Manitoba was rated below average. June temperatures in western Ontario were cooler than normal, and precipitation above average, and normal production was expected.

Northern Alberta, Northeastern British Columbia, and Northwest Territories: In northern Alberta, northeastern British Columbia, and the Northwest Territories (strata 13-18, 20, 75-77), spring was late, especially in the eastern area of the unit. Biologists reported that large numbers of ducks apparently over-flew the dry prairies. Most birds were concentrated on the open wetlands on the west side of the survey area, and had fewer opportunities to nest on the east side, especially the early-nesting species. The spring thaw came too late to benefit

most early-nesting species, but was right on schedule for the later-nesting species. Breeding conditions should also be excellent for scoters. Total-duck, mallard, northern pintail, and scaup numbers were similar to 2003 counts ($P\geq0.160$), but remained 19%, 30%, 50%, and 39% below their long-term averages, respectively ($P<0.001$). Blue-winged teal did not differ from their 2003 counts ($P=0.389$), but remained 49% above their long-term average ($P=0.087$). Gadwall (+82% above 2003, +211% above LTA) and redhead (+150% above 2003, +97% above LTA) numbers were higher than last year's estimates and their long-term averages ($P\geq0.066$). Green-winged teal, northern shoveler, and canvasback estimates were similar to those of 2003 and to long-term averages ($P\geq0.141$).

Although much of northern Alberta and northeastern British Columbia experienced a very late spring, temperatures have been normal since mid-June, though precipitation was 50% below normal. As of July, production potential was rated fair to good throughout stratum 20 and in stratum 77 west of the Birch and Caribou Mountains. In the northeastern portion of stratum 77 that experienced a record late spring, production should be poor to fair.

Alaska, Yukon Territory, and Old Crow Flats: In Alaska, the Yukon Territory, and Old Crow Flats (strata 1-12), breeding conditions depend largely on the timing of spring phenology, because wetland conditions are less variable than on the prairies. In general, this region experienced an early spring breakup, with the exception of the North Slope. Areas south of the Brooks Range experienced a widespread, record-setting early spring breakup. Snow and ice melt, and greening of vegetation occurred rapidly, with only minor flooding. Conditions on the Old Crow Flats in the Yukon appeared more normal. Estimates of all duck species were similar to those of 2003, with the exception of green-winged teal, which were 21% below their 2003 count ($P=0.068$), but 140% above their long-term average ($P<0.001$). Total duck (+57%), mallard (+138%), American wigeon (+81%), and northern shoveler estimates (+156%) were all higher than their long-term averages ($P<0.001$). Gadwall, blue-winged teal, northern pintail, redhead, canvasback, and scaup populations all remained similar to their long-term averages ($P\geq0.121$).

Warm temperatures and moisture across much of Alaska during June and July and minimal flooding largely maintained the excellent conditions observed by biologists in May. Overall, excellent production is anticipated for most of

Alaska, with good conditions prevailing on the Old Crow Flats. The interior boreal forest experienced warm temperatures with little moisture, and experienced the third-worst wildfire season on record. This may have negatively affected waterfowl production.

Eastern Survey Area: Breeding habitat conditions were generally good to excellent in the eastern U.S. and Canada (strata 51-56 and 62-69). Timing of the spring thaw was normal in Maine and conditions were excellent there and in the Maritime Provinces and Newfoundland, but late in Labrador, where nesting was delayed for birds at higher elevations and production potential was rated good. Production may be somewhat adversely affected in parts of Labrador, where snow and ice persisted into June, but otherwise should be normal for this region. Much of central and southern Quebec experienced a long, cold, dry winter, and a dry spring. Despite the lack of precipitation, wetlands were sufficiently abundant and in adequate condition, and most areas were rated good. Below-average temperatures persisted through July and substantial June rainfall caused some flooding. The southwestern portion of the province was drier, and habitat there was fair to good. The production outlook for Quebec is normal to slightly below normal. Spring weather in southern Ontario was variable, as initially cool temperatures gave way to mild weather. Wetlands in southern Ontario and along the St. Lawrence Valley were in generally good condition.

Following the survey, several weeks of severe spring thunderstorms led to flooding in portions of southwestern Ontario, which may have negatively impacted early nests there. Good wetland conditions persisted in southern Ontario and the St. Lawrence Valley of Ontario through July. Production there is expected to be normal this year. Spring was slightly delayed in central Ontario, but wetlands were in good condition and production should be normal. Spring was also slightly delayed in the western James Bay Lowlands of Ontario; however, the survey in late May revealed little remaining lake ice, good water conditions, and well-distributed birds. The production outlook for this region was normal. The ring-necked duck population estimate in May was 67% above the 2003 estimate ($P=0.095$), but similar to the long-term average ($P=0.225$). American wigeon and goldeneyes were similar to their 2003 estimates ($P\geq0.133$), but were 61% ($P=0.004$) and 42% ($P=0.052$) below their long-term averages. None of the other species, or the total duck estimate,

differed from 2003 estimates or long-term averages ($P\geq0.133$).

Other areas: Conditions were dry in many areas along the West Coast of the U.S. and Canada. Breeding habitat conditions in British Columbia were the worst on record, as indicated by the greatest number of dry or partially dry wetlands within the survey area, and the lowest numbers of total ducks and mallards recorded since the survey began in 1988. Mild temperatures and low precipitation during late winter produced a gradual snow thaw that reduced runoff and led to poor wetland conditions. Approximately 6,300 ducks were observed in British Columbia's annual survey, which was similar to the 2003 count and the long-term average ($P\geq0.277$). Mallard numbers were 27% below the long-term average ($P=0.015$). Conditions were also dry in Washington, and pothole numbers were down 35% from 2003 and were 36% below the long-term average because the pothole region did not receive the snowmelt runoff it needed to fill basins. The 2004 total-duck estimate in Washington was 114,900, down 10% from last year and 28% below the long-term average. Mallards were up slightly from 39,800 in 2003 to 40,000 in 2004, but remain 27% below the long-term average. In California, winter precipitation was average, but spring was dry in most of the state. Good conditions prevailed in the northeastern part of the state, where good production was expected. Elsewhere, duck nesting effort will likely be lower than normal. The total-duck estimate was 412,800, 23% lower than last year's ($P=0.079$), and 31% below the long-term average ($P<0.001$). Mallards (262,400) were not significantly different from their 2003 estimate but were 30% below their long-term average ($P<0.003$). In Oregon, similar trends existed for estimates of total ducks and mallards. Both were similar to those of 2003 ($P\geq0.563$), but were 16% and 21% below their long-term averages, respectively ($P\geq0.042$).

Conditions were also generally dry in the interior-western U.S. In Nebraska, the dry conditions which began in 2001 and 2002 continued into the fall and winter of 2003-2004. In the spring of 2004, biologists counted the lowest number of water areas since standard survey methods were implemented in 1999. This was also the lowest count for mallards, blue-winged teal, gadwall, and pintail. The estimated breeding population of ducks of almost 70,000 birds was 27% below the 2003 estimate and 61% below the 1999-2003 average. Nevada suffered its fourth year of drought; many wetlands were dry, as were two complete river systems. Nonetheless, duck numbers were up. This increase in duck numbers may reflect the timing of the survey or birds being compressed onto the few remaining wetlands. Total ducks numbered 24,200, compared to 21,100 in 2003. At 1,700, mallard numbers were similar to the 2003 count. Duck breeding habitat conditions were still poor to fair in southern and eastern Wyoming, but spring precipitation improved conditions in northeast Wyoming. Conditions in Colorado were improved over 2003, but were still only fair. Cool, wet weather in the late spring may have delayed nesting. Overall, only fair to poor duck production is expected from Colorado this year.

Habitats around the Great Lakes were also somewhat dry in the spring, but seemed to be in better shape than those to the west, especially after many received abundant rain during the late spring. In Minnesota, pond numbers declined 19% relative to 2003, and were 20% below the 1968-2003 average. Mallard numbers (375,300) were statistically similar to the 2003 estimate. At 353,200, blue-winged teal were 83% higher than the 2003 estimate (P=0.02), and 54% above the long-term average. Total ducks numbered 1,008,300, up 40% from 2003, 20% higher than the 10-year average, and 60% above the long-term average. During the Wisconsin waterfowl survey (April 27-May 7) conditions were dry and wetland numbers were below the long-term mean. However, abundant rain beginning in late May and continuing into June improved wetland conditions. Wisconsin total duck numbers were 22% higher than the 2003 estimate and 58% above the 1973-2003 average. Mallard numbers were 12% below the 2003 level, but 32% above the long-term mean. In Michigan, the total duck estimate was 20% higher than last year's. Mallard numbers did not differ from last year's count, but remained 25% below the long-term average (P=0.054).

In the Atlantic Flyway states along the East Coast of the U.S., habitat conditions for nesting waterfowl were good again this year. Normal to above-normal late-winter and early-spring rains kept wetlands full, providing ample nesting habitat. Variable weather made for variable nest initiation dates. Late-spring rains likely helped waterfowl broods in the southern portion of this region, but coupled with cool temperatures in the northern portions, may have reduced brood survival there. Total duck and mallard numbers from the Atlantic Flyway's Breeding Waterfowl survey were similar to the 2003 estimates ($P\geq$0.313), and to their long-term averages ($P\geq$0.854).

Mallard Fall-flight Index

The mid-continent mallard population is composed of mallards from the traditional survey area, Michigan, Minnesota, and Wisconsin, and is 8.4 ± 0.3

million (Fig. 3). This is similar to the 2003 estimate of 8.8 ± 0.4 million (P=0.289). The 2004 mid-continent mallard fall-flight index is 9.4 ± 0.1 million, statistically similar to the 2003 estimate of 10.3 ± 0.1 million birds (P=0.467). These indices were based on revised mid-continent mallard population models, and therefore, differ from those previously published (USFWS Adaptive Harvest Management Report 2004, Runge et al. 2002).

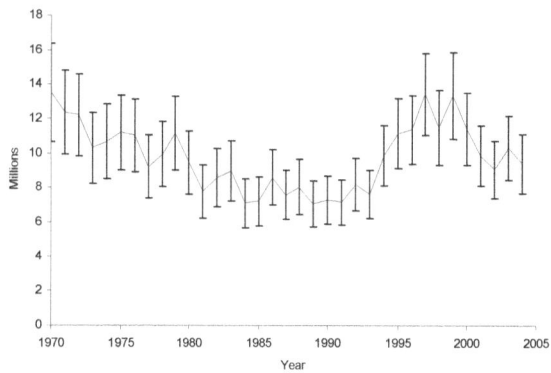

Fig. 3. Estimates and 95% confidence intervals for the size of the mallard population in the fall.

REFERENCES

Drought Watch on the Prairies, 2004. Agriculture and Agri-Food Canada. (www.agr.ca/pfra/drought.htm).

Environment Canada, 2004. Climate Trends and Variations Bulletin. Green Lane Internet Publication,Downsview,ON. (www1.tor.ec.gc.ca/ccrm/bulletin/).

NOAA/USDA Joint Agriculture Weather Facility. 2004. Weekly Weather and Crop Bulletin. Washington, DC.(www.usda.gov/oce/waob/jawf).

Runge, M. C., F. A. Johnson, J. A. Dubovsky, W. L. Kendall, J. Lawrence, J. Gammonley. 2002. A revised protocol for the Adaptive Harvest Management of Mid-Continent Mallards. (migratorybirds.fws.gov/reports/ahm02/MCMrevise2002.pdf)

Sauer, J.R., and S. Droege. 1990. Wood duck population trends from the North American Breeding Bird Survey. Pages 159-165 in L.H. Frederickson, G. V. Burger, S.P. Havera, D.A. Graber, R.E. Kirby, and T.S. Taylor, eds. Proceedings of the 1988 North American Wood Duck Symposium, St. Louis, MO.

U.S. Fish and Wildlife Service. 2004. Adaptive Harvest Management: 2004 Duck Hunting Season. U.S. Dept. Interior, Washington, D.C. 35pp. U.S. Fish and Wildlife Service. 2004. Waterfowl Population Survey Section area reports.

Wilkins, K. A., and M. C. Otto. 2004. Trends in duck breeding populations, 1955-2004. U.S. Dept. Interior, Washington, D.C. 19pp.

STATUS OF GEESE AND SWANS

Abstract: We provide information on the population status and productivity of North American Canada geese (*Branta canadensis*), brant (*B. bernicla*), snow geese (*Chen caerulescens*), Ross's geese (*C. rossii*), emperor geese (*C. canagica*), white-fronted geese (*Anser albifrons*) and tundra swans *(Cygnus columbianus).* The timing of spring snowmelt in northern goose and swan nesting areas varied in 2004 from very early in western Alaska to very late in areas near Hudson Bay and in northern Quebec. Reproductive success of geese and swans in areas that experienced near-average spring phenology might have been reduced by persistent snow cover and harsh conditions that encompassed a large expanse of migration and staging habitat. Of the 26 populations for which current primary population indices were available, 7 populations (Atlantic Population, Aleutian, and 3 temperate-nesting populations of Canada geese; Pacific Population white-fronted geese; and Eastern Population tundra swans) displayed significant positive trends, and only Short Grass Prairie Population Canada geese displayed a significant negative trend over the most recent 10-year period. The forecast for production of geese and swans in North America in 2004 is improved from 2003 in the Pacific Flyway, but generally similar to, or lower than, 2003 for the remainder of North America.

This section summarizes information regarding the status, annual production of young, and expected fall flights of goose and tundra swan populations in North America. Information was compiled from a broad geographic area and is provided to assist managers in regulating harvest. We have used the most widely accepted nomenclature for various waterfowl populations, but they may differ from other published information. Some of the goose populations described herein are comprised of more than 1 subspecies and some light goose populations contain lesser snow geese and Ross's geese.

Most populations of geese and swans in North America nest in the Arctic or subarctic regions of Alaska and Canada (Fig. 1), but several Canada goose populations nest in temperate regions of the United States and southern Canada ("temperate-nesting" populations). Populations are monitored by various methods on breeding, migration, or wintering areas. The annual production of young by northern-nesting geese is influenced greatly by weather conditions on the breeding grounds, especially the timing of spring snowmelt and its impact on the initiation of nesting activity (i.e., phenology). Persistent snow cover reduces nest site availability, delays nesting activity, and often results in depressed reproductive effort and productivity. In general, goose productivity will be better than average if nesting begins by late May in western and central portions of the Arctic, and by early June in the eastern Arctic. Production usually is poor if nest initiations are delayed much beyond 15 June. For temperate-nesting Canada goose populations, recruitment rates are less variable, but productivity is influenced by localized drought and flood events.

METHODS

Population estimates for geese are derived from a variety of surveys conducted by biologists from federal, state, and provincial agencies, and universities (Appendices B, J, and K). Surveys include the Midwinter Survey (MWS, conducted each January in wintering areas), the Breeding Population and Habitat Survey (BPHS, see Duck section of this report), surveys specifically designed for various populations, and others. When survey methodology allowed, 95% confidence intervals were presented with population estimates. The 10-year trends of population estimates were calculated through regression of the natural logarithm of survey results on year, and slope coefficients were presented and tested for equality to zero (*t*-test). Changes in population indices between the current and previous years were calculated, and, where possible, assessed with a *z*-test using the sum of sampling variances for the 2 estimates. Primary population indices, those related to population objectives, are described first in population-specific sections.

Due to the completion of this report prior to final field assessment of goose and swan reproduction, the annual productivity of most goose populations can only be predicted qualitatively. Information on habitat conditions and forecasts of productivity were based primarily on information from various waterfowl surveys and interviews with field biologists. These reports provide reliable information for specific locations but may not provide accurate assessment for the vast geographic range of waterfowl populations.

Fig. 1. Important goose nesting areas in Arctic and subarctic North America.

RESULTS AND DISCUSSION

Conditions in the Arctic and Subarctic

Spring phenology varied widely throughout North America in 2004. The Yukon-Kuskokwim Delta and much of the rest of Alaska reported a very early spring snowmelt, minimal flooding, and favorable conditions for nesting geese. In contrast, snow cover was very persistent near Hudson Bay, the Ungava Peninsula, and a broad expanse of migration and staging habitats across Canada's boreal forest. The snow and ice cover graphic (Fig. 2, National Oceanic and Atmospheric Administration) illustrates the more extensive snow cover across Canada's subarctic region this year compared with 2003.

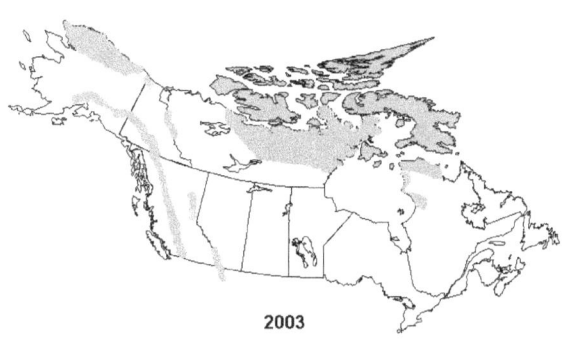

2003

2004

Fig. 2. The extent of snow and ice cover in North America on 2 June 2003 and 2 June 2004 (data from National Oceanic and Atmospheric Administration).

Conditions in Southern Canada and the United States

Conditions that influence the productivity of Canada geese vary less from year to year in these temperate regions than in the Arctic and subarctic. Given adequate wetland numbers and the absence of flood events, temperate-nesting Canada geese are reliably productive. In the spring of 2004, wetland abundance and condition in many western states remained depressed from drought. Well-below average wetland abundance in the Canadian prairies in 2004 may have reduced goose productivity there. Most temperate-nesting Canada goose populations, with the exception of the Pacific and Rocky Mountain Populations, likely experienced average or above average production in 2004.

Status of Canada Geese

North Atlantic Population (NAP): NAP Canada geese principally nest in Newfoundland and Labrador. They generally commingle during winter with other Atlantic Flyway Canada geese, although NAP geese have a more coastal distribution than other populations (Fig. 3).

During the 2004 BPHS, biologists estimated 67,800 (± 34,500) indicated pairs (singles plus pairs) in NAP range (strata 66 and 67), 12% higher (*P*=0.758) than in 2003 (Fig. 4). Indicated pair estimates have declined an average of 3% per year since surveys were initiated in 1996 (*P*=0.289). A total of 197,200 (± 115,200) Canada geese were estimated during the BPHS, 48% higher than last year's estimate (*P*=0.341). Total goose estimates have declined an average of 2% per year during 1996-2004 (*P*=0.419). The pair density determined by the 2004 expanded CWS helicopter plot survey was 18% higher than the 2001-2003 average. Spring conditions were favorable for geese in Newfoundland and lower elevations of Labrador. A fall flight somewhat larger than that produced in 2003 is expected.

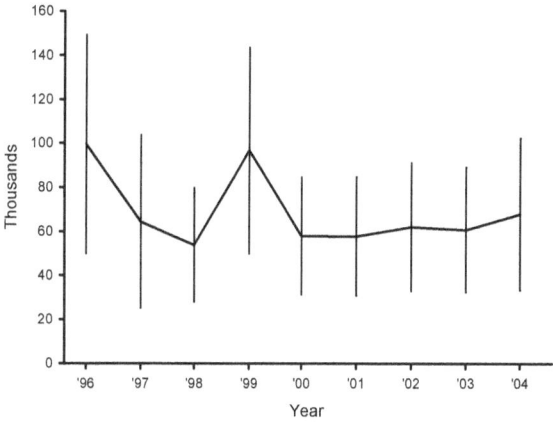

Fig. 4. Estimated number (and 95% confidence intervals) of North Atlantic Population Canada geese breeding pairs during spring.

Atlantic Population (AP): AP Canada geese nest throughout much of Quebec, especially along Ungava Bay, the eastern shore of Hudson Bay, and

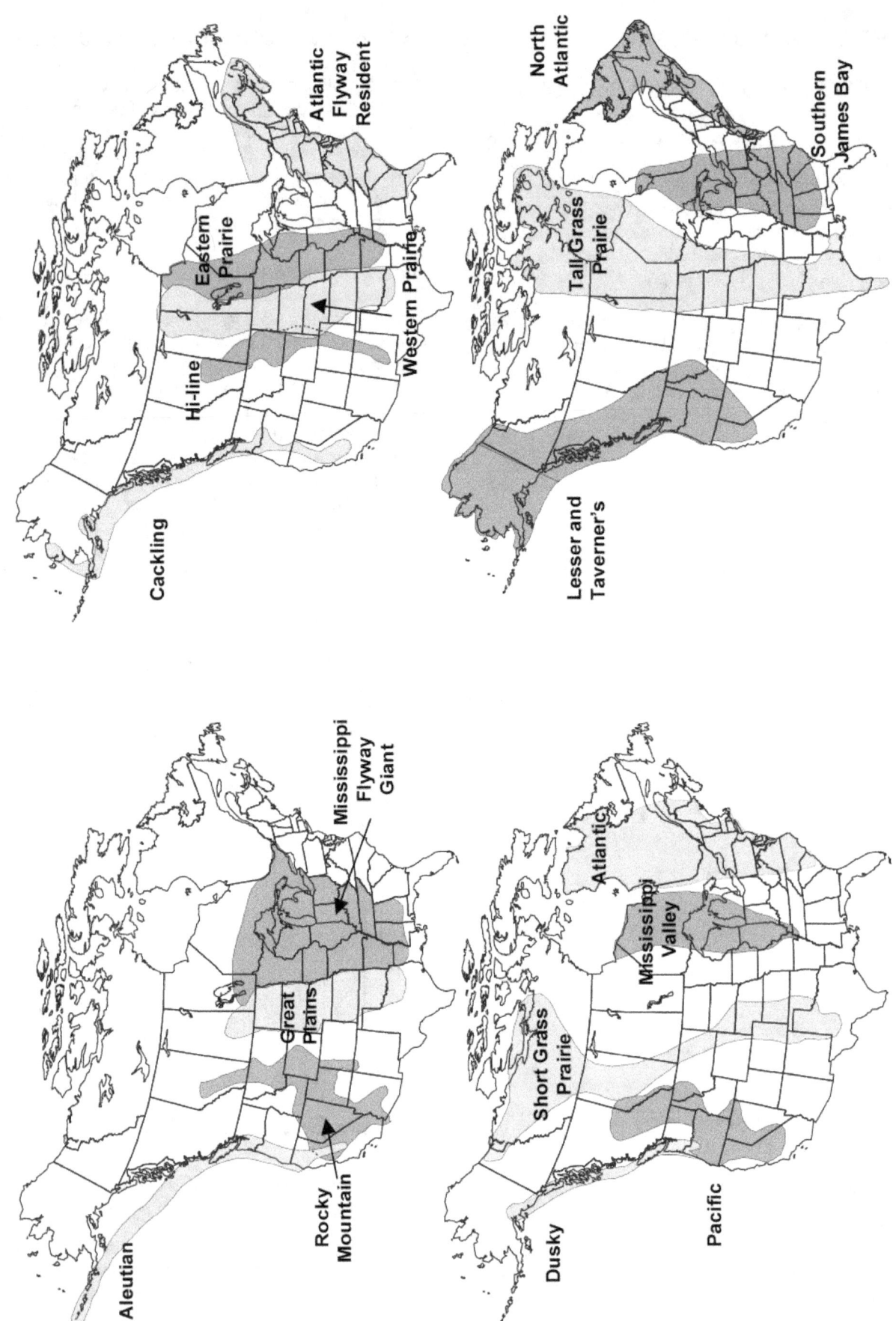

Fig. 3. Approximate ranges of Canada goose populations in North America.

on the Ungava Peninsula. The AP winters from New England to South Carolina, but the largest concentrations occur on the Delmarva Peninsula (Fig. 3).

AP surveys in 2004 estimated 174,800 (± 29,500) indicated breeding pairs, 11% more than last year (P=0.358, Fig. 5). This population has increased from a low of 29,000 breeding pairs in 1995. The breeding pair estimates have increased an average of 20% per year during 1995-2004 (P<0.001). The estimated total spring population of 1,014,600 (± 167,700) geese in 2004 was 33% higher than last year (P=0.39) but likely was inflated by the presence of many molt migrants. Spring phenology was delayed by cold May temperatures and persistent snow cover throughout much of the northern AP range. The proportion of indicated pairs observed as singles (34%) was the lowest recorded since 1993 (mean=49%), suggesting a poor nesting effort. The number of nests found on Hudson Bay study sites was reduced 34%, and mean clutch size was reduced 28% from 2003. At Ungava Bay study areas, nesting effort was also reduced substantially, clutch size was lower, and nest-destruction rates were higher compared to last year. A fall flight somewhat smaller than last year is expected.

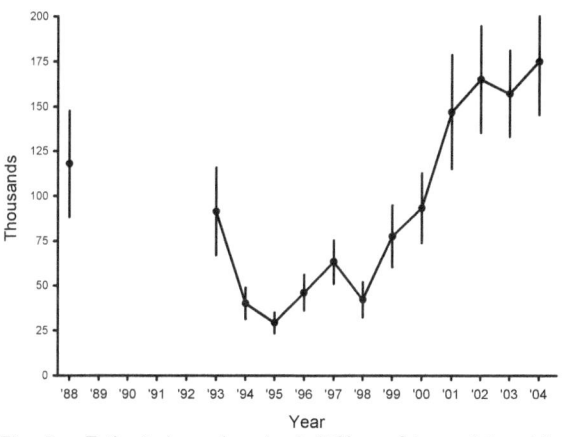

Fig. 5. Estimated number (and 95% confidence intervals) of Atlantic Population Canada goose breeding pairs in northern Quebec.

Atlantic Flyway Resident Population (AFRP): This population of large Canada geese inhabits southern Quebec, the southern Maritime provinces, and all states of the Atlantic Flyway (Fig. 3).

Spring surveys in 2004 in AFRP range indicated there were 980,400 (± 176,400) Canada geese in this population (Fig. 6), about 10% fewer than in 2003 (P=0.424). These estimates have increased an average of 2% per year over the last 10 years (P=0.049). Nesting conditions in most states were favorable and production was expected to be above

average. A large fall flight, similar to last year's is expected.

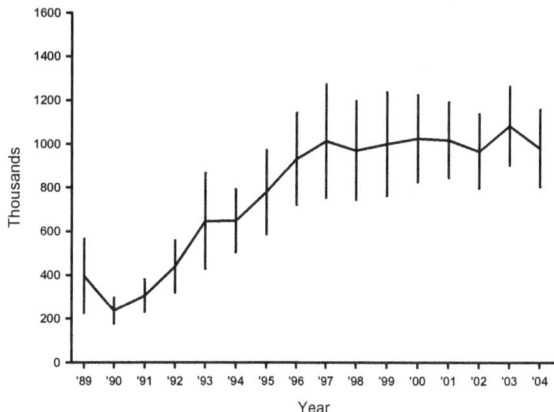

Fig. 6. Estimated number (and 95% confidence intervals) of Atlantic Flyway Resident Population Canada geese during spring.

Southern James Bay Population (SJBP): This population nests on Akimiski Island and in the Hudson Bay Lowlands to the west and south of James Bay. The SJBP winters from southern Ontario and Michigan to Mississippi, Alabama, Georgia, and South Carolina (Fig. 3).

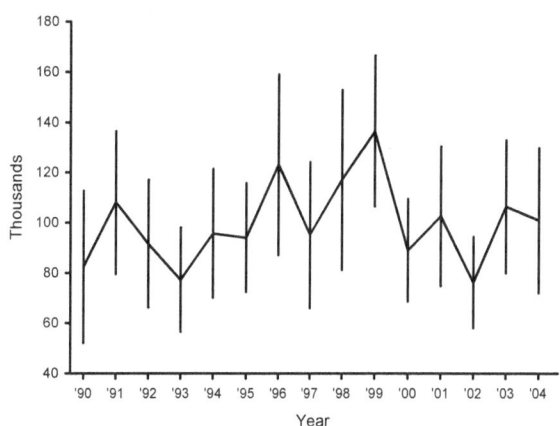

Fig. 7. Estimated total population (and 95% confidence intervals) of Southern James Bay Population Canada geese during spring.

Breeding ground surveys indicated a spring population of 101,000 (± 29,000) Canada geese in 2004, 5% lower than last year (P=0.785, Fig. 7). These estimates have decreased an average of 1% per year since 1995 (P=0.488). In 2004, surveys estimated 37,600 (± 11,700) breeding pairs, 16% fewer than in 2003 (P=0.339) and a record low on Akimiski Island. Surveyors indicated molt migrants likely were not a factor in this year's survey. Cold temperatures in April and early May delayed snowmelt and goose nest initiation in SJBP range, especially north of the Albany River. On Akimiski Island, nesting phenology was the second latest on record, total nest loss was high (41.3%), and estimated clutch size and the number of goslings leaving nests was the lowest recorded since nest monitoring began in 1993. Although conditions in other portions of the SJBP breeding range may not have been as severe as on Akimiski, a fall flight smaller than that of 2003 is expected.

Mississippi Valley Population (MVP): The principal nesting range of this population is in northern Ontario, especially in the Hudson Bay Lowlands, west of Hudson and James Bays. MVP Canada geese primarily concentrate during fall and winter in Wisconsin, Illinois, and Michigan (Fig. 3).

Breeding ground surveys conducted in 2004 indicated a total population of 727,000 ($\pm$ 153,800) MVP Canada geese, a 37% increase from last spring (*P*=0.049, Fig. 8). There is little trend in these estimates since 1995 (1%, *P*=0.754). The presence of molt migrant Canada geese likely inflated the total goose estimate in 2004. Biologists estimated there were 138,200 ($\pm$ 30,700) nests in 2004, 23% fewer than in 2003 (*P*=0.104) and the second lowest number recorded since 1989. Estimates of MVP nests have declined an average of 3% per year during 1995-2004 (*P*=0.134). Cold temperatures in April and May left the coast of Hudson Bay between Winisk and Cape Henrietta-Maria 95% snow covered in late May. Conditions delayed the estimated peak of hatch to June 30, the latest observed since nesting studies were initiated in 1985. At Burntpoint Creek, nest density was reduced by 74% compared with 2003. Reduced nesting effort, low clutch sizes, and cold and wet weather during incubation and early brood rearing will contribute to poor production in 2004. A fall flight reduced from 2003 is expected.

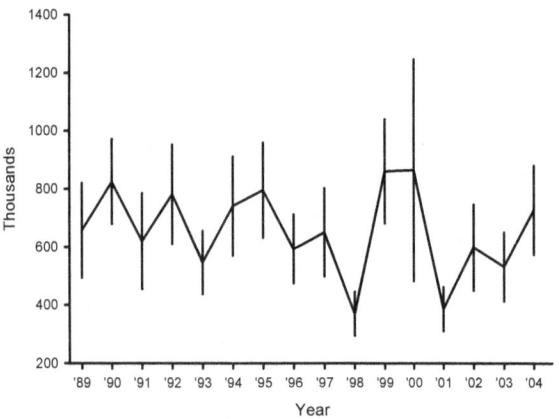

Fig. 8. Estimated number (and 95% confidence intervals) of Mississippi Valley Population Canada geese during spring.

Mississippi Flyway Giant Population (MFGP): Giant Canada geese have been reestablished or introduced in all Mississippi Flyway states. This large subspecies now represents a significant portion of all Canada geese in the Mississippi Flyway (Fig. 3).

This population has been monitored with spring surveys since 1993. In 2004, the preliminary population estimate was 1,582,200, 3% lower than the final 2003 estimate of 1,633,000 (Fig. 9). These estimates have increased an average of 6% per year since 1995 (*P*<0.001). Although nesting conditions were suboptimal in Iowa and Tennessee, most states expected average or above average production in 2004. Another large fall flight is expected.

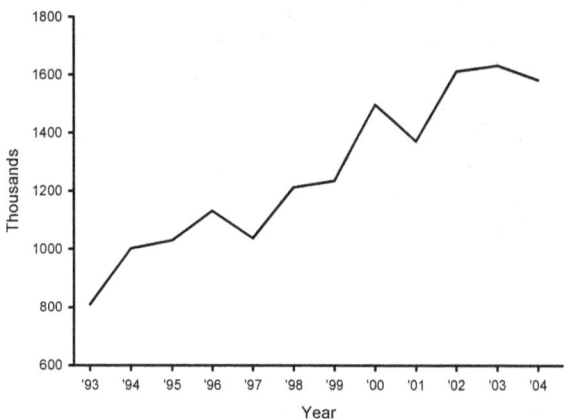

Fig. 9. Estimated number of Mississippi Flyway Giant Population Canada geese during spring.

Eastern Prairie Population (EPP): These geese nest in the Hudson Bay Lowlands of Manitoba and concentrate primarily in Manitoba, Minnesota, and Missouri during winter (Fig. 3).

The 2004 spring estimate of EPP geese was 290,700 ($\pm$ 36,800), 27% larger than the 2003 estimate (*P*=0.015, Fig. 10). Spring estimates have increased an average of 4% per year over the last 10 years (*P*=0.101). The 2004 estimate of singles and pairs was 145,500 ($\pm$ 19,800), 18% higher than last year (*P*=0.091). There is no trend in these estimates during 1995-2004. However, the estimate of productive geese (singles and nesting pairs), 48,100, declined (*P*=0.001) from 2003 to the second lowest value record since 1984. May temperatures in EPP range were the lowest on record since 1976. May temperature data and delayed nest initiation indicate a "bust" in production for EPP geese. This year, biologists at Nestor One observed the latest median hatch date (11 July), the lowest nest density (0.008/ha), and lowest mean clutch size (2.2 eggs) recorded during 1976-2004. A fall flight lower than 2003, including few young is expected.

28

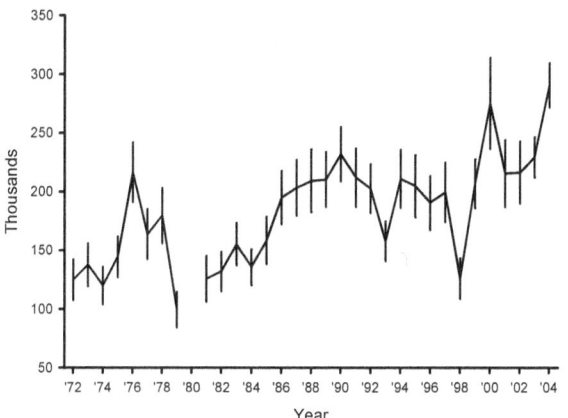

Fig. 10. Estimated number (and 95% confidence intervals) of Eastern Prairie Population Canada geese during spring.

Western Prairie and Great Plains Populations (WPP/GPP): The WPP is composed of mid-sized and large Canada geese that nest in eastern Saskatchewan and western Manitoba. The GPP is composed of large Canada geese resulting from restoration efforts in Saskatchewan, North Dakota, South Dakota, Nebraska, Kansas, Oklahoma, and Texas. Geese from these breeding populations commingle during migration with other Canada geese along the Missouri River in the Dakotas and on reservoirs from southwestern Kansas to Texas (Fig. 3). These 2 populations are managed jointly and surveyed during winter.

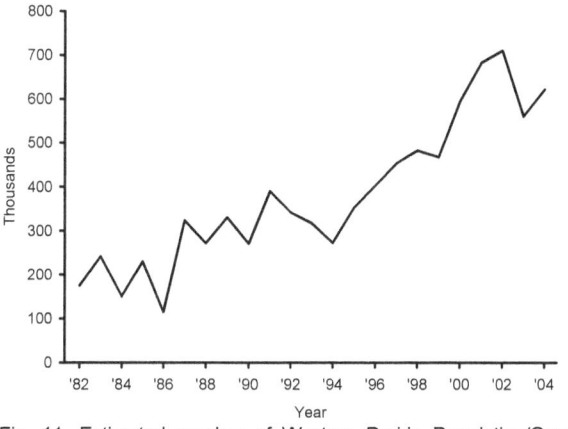

Fig. 11. Estimated number of Western Prairie Population/Great Plains Population Canada geese during winter.

During the 2004 MWS survey, 622,100 WPP/GPP geese were counted, 11% more than the 2003 index (Fig. 11). These indices have increased an average of 7% per year since 1995 (P=0.001). A 2004 index of the spring population in a portion of WPP/GPP range from the BPHS was 690,000 ($\pm$ 123,800), 4% larger than last year (P=0.749). The BPHS estimates have also increased an average of 7% per year since

1995 (P<0.001). Goose production in the northeastern portion of WPP range likely was reduced by a delayed spring snowmelt similar to that experienced within EPP range. Wetland abundance in southern Saskatchewan, Manitoba, and in Oklahoma was below average but other states reported favorable nesting conditions. A heavy snow in mid-May in the U.S. and Canadian prairies may have impacted production. A fall flight similar to last year's is expected.

Tall Grass Prairie Population (TGPP): These small Canada geese nest on Baffin (particularly on the Great Plain of the Koukdjuak), Southampton, and King William Islands; north of the Maguse and McConnell Rivers on the Hudson Bay coast; and in the eastern Queen Maud Gulf region. TGPP Canada geese winter mainly in Oklahoma, Texas, and northeastern Mexico (Fig. 3). These geese mix with other Canada geese on wintering areas, making it difficult to estimate the size of the population.

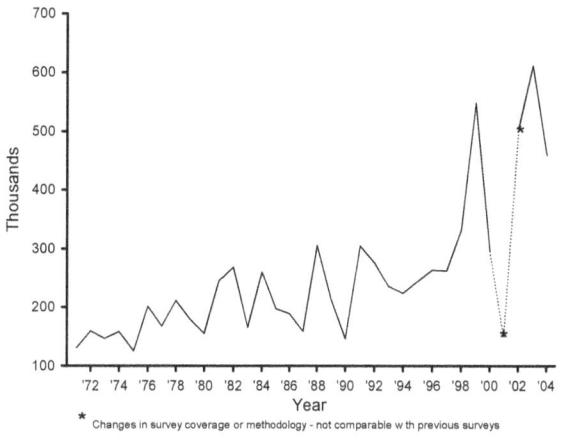

* Changes in survey coverage or methodology - not comparable with previous surveys

Fig. 12. Estimated number of Tall Grass Prairie Population Canada geese in the Central Flyway during winter.

During the 2004 MWS in the Central Flyway, 458,700 TGPP geese were tallied, 25% fewer than in 2003 (Fig. 12). These estimates have increased an average of 7% per year during 1995-2004 (P=0.151). Spring breakup near the McConnell River, Northwest Territories was delayed by nearly 3 weeks. Limited information suggests that spring phenology on Southampton and Baffin Islands was later than in 2003 but near or only slightly later than average. Important nesting areas were snow-free on 17 June and 24 June on Baffin and Southampton Island, respectively. In the Queen Maud Gulf spring snow melt occurred earlier than average but goose arrival was delayed, perhaps due to the persistent snow cover on more southerly staging areas. Biologists on Southampton Island indicated that snow goose nesting effort appeared to be reduced from 2003, and on Baffin Island a sample of snow goose clutch sizes were slightly smaller than in 2003. Limited information suggests production of TGPP Canada geese will be below that of 2003.

Short Grass Prairie Population (SGPP): These small Canada geese nest on Victoria and Jenny Lind Islands and on the mainland from the Queen Maud Gulf west and south to the Mackenzie River and northern Alberta. These geese winter in southeastern Colorado, northeastern New Mexico, and the Oklahoma and Texas panhandles (Fig. 3).

During the 2004 MWS, biologists counted 203,600 SGPP Canada geese, 30% more than in 2003 (Fig. 13). These indices have declined 17% per year since 1995 ($P<0.001$). A portion of the SGPP breeding range in the Northwest Territories is covered by the BPHS (strata 13-18). The 2004 BPHS estimated 97,500 ($\pm$ 36,400) SGPP geese, a 14% increase from 2003 ($P=0.642$). These estimates show no trend during 1995-2004 ($P=0.903$). Spring snowmelt was earlier than average near Queen Maud Gulf but goose arrival was delayed, apparently by the persistent snow cover in a broad strip from the Mackenzie River mouth to the Hudson Bay coast. Nesting phenology of Canada geese and light geese are influenced by many of the same factors. Nest initiations of light geese at Karrak Lake in 2004 were about 8 days later than average and clutch sizes were slightly below the long-term mean. Surveys on Victoria Island indicated a good Canada goose nesting effort there. Spring phenology on the mainland of the western Canadian Arctic was delayed and breeding success there will likely be reduced. With limited specific information, production from SGPP geese is expected to be no better than average.

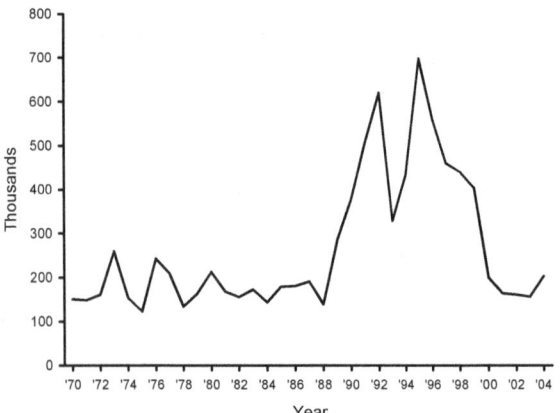

Fig. 13. Estimated number of Short Grass Prairie Population Canada geese during winter.

Hi-line Population (HLP): These large Canada geese nest in southeastern Alberta, southwestern Saskatchewan, eastern Montana and Wyoming, and in Colorado. They winter in Colorado and in central New Mexico (Fig. 3).

The 2004 MWS indicated a total of 215,600 HLP Canada geese, which is 5% more than last year's estimate (Fig. 14). The MWS estimates have increased an average of 4% per year since 1995 ($P=0.128$). An estimate of the spring population was obtained from the 2004 BPHS in areas of Saskatchewan, Alberta, and Montana. The BPHS estimate was 200,500 ($\pm$ 50,100), 13% lower than the 2003 estimate ($P=0.470$). These population estimates have also increased 4% per year since 1994 ($P=0.128$). Wetland abundance in southern Saskatchewan and Alberta in 2004 declined substantially from 2003 and the long-term average, and much of Montana and Wyoming remained in drought. The fall flight of HLP geese is expected to be similar to that of last year.

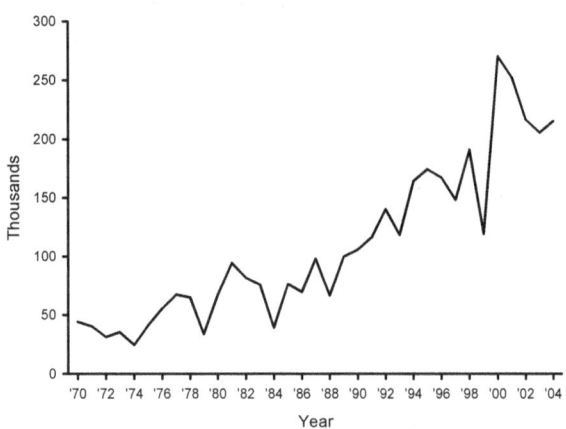

Fig. 14. Estimated number of Hi-line Population Canada geese during winter.

Rocky Mountain Population (RMP): These large Canada geese nest in southern Alberta and western Montana, and the inter-mountain regions of Utah, Idaho, Nevada, Wyoming, and Colorado. They winter mainly in central and southern California, Arizona, Nevada, Utah, Idaho, and Montana (Fig. 3).

The estimated spring population derived from the BPHS in 2004 was 152,500 ($\pm$ 53,800), 13% higher than last year's estimate ($P=0.590$). The BPHS estimates have increased 3% per year during the last 10 years ($P=0.062$). During the 2004 MWS (no survey conducted in Idaho this year), 111,600 geese were counted, 11% fewer than in 2003 (Fig. 15). MWS estimates have shown no trend since 1995 ($P=0.376$). Wetland abundance in southern Alberta declined substantially from 2003 and the long-term average, and much of RMP range remained in drought. In contrast, numbers of breeding pairs and production in Utah are above long-term averages, and near the most recent 10-year average. The fall flight of RMP geese is expected to be similar to last year's.

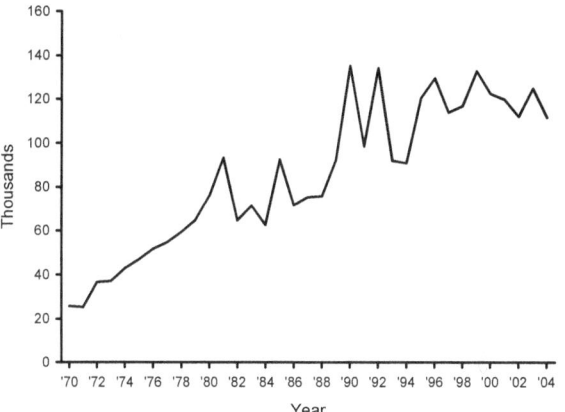

Fig. 15. Estimated number of Rocky Mountain Population Canada geese during winter.

Pacific Population (PP): These large Canada geese nest and winter west of the Rocky Mountains from northern Alberta and British Columbia south through the Pacific Northwest to California (Fig. 3).

The BPHS index of PP geese in Alberta (strata 76-77) was 59,300 in 2004, 23% lower than in 2003 (P=0.480). These estimates have increased an average of 5% per year since 1995 (P=0.138). Most PP breeding areas remain under drought conditions but average or better production was reported in portions of Oregon and northeast California. Wetland abundance in the range of the PP continues to be reduced by drought. Predictions of PP production or fall flight cannot be reliably made without more information.

Dusky Canada Geese: These mid-sized Canada geese predominantly nest on the Copper River Delta of southeastern Alaska, and winter principally in the Willamette and Lower Columbia River Valleys of Oregon and Washington (Fig. 3).

The size of the population is estimated through observations of marked geese during December and January. The 2003-2004 population estimate was 14,900 ($\pm$ 3,500), 11% lower than in 2002-2003 (P=0.475, Fig. 16). These estimates have increased an average 6% per year during the last 10-year period (P=0.900). Preliminary results from the 2004 spring survey of the Copper River Delta indicated the index of total dusky Canada geese increased 4%, and singles and pairs increased 23% from last year's levels. Both estimates remain below the 1986-2003 average. The Copper River Delta experienced a

warm spring, with snowmelt about 1 week earlier than average. Nesting phenology was early and an extended euchalon run reduced bald eagle predation on dusky geese. A fall flight higher than last year is expected.

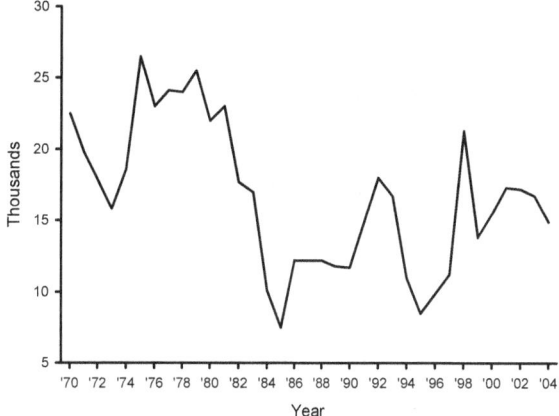

Fig. 16. Estimated number of dusky Canada geese during winter.

Cackling Canada Geese: Cackling Canada geese nest on the Yukon-Kuskokwim Delta (YKD) of western Alaska. They primarily winter in the Willamette and Lower Columbia River Valleys of Oregon and Washington (Fig. 3).

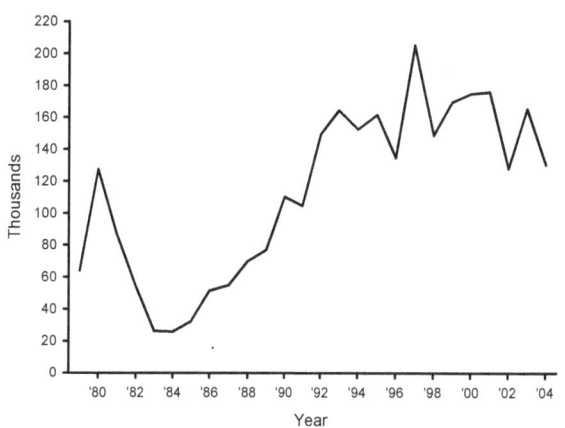

Fig. 17. Number of cackling Canada geese estimated from fall and spring surveys.

The index used for this population was a fall estimate from 1979-1998. Since 1999, the index has been an estimate of the fall population derived from spring counts of adults on the YKD. The 2004 fall estimate is 130,200, 21% lower than in 2003. These estimates have decreased an average of 1% per year since 1995 (P=0.435, Fig. 17). Surveys in the coastal zone of the YKD during spring 2004 indicated little change in single and paired cackling geese, and a decrease of 27% in total birds from 2003 estimates. An early spring snowmelt led to advanced nesting

31

phenology in 2004. Estimated hatching dates for cackling geese were 12 days earlier than average and the earliest since 1982. YKD nesting surveys indicated increases in nest numbers, mean clutch size, and nest success. With the good production outlook this year, a fall flight exceeding last year's is expected.

Lesser and *Taverner's* *Canada* *Geese:* These subspecies nest throughout much of interior and south-central Alaska and winter in Washington, Oregon, and California (Fig. 3). Taverner's geese are more associated with the North Slope and tundra areas, while lesser Canada geese tend to nest in Alaska's interior. However, these subspecies mix with other Canada geese throughout the year and reliable estimates of separate populations are not presently available.

The estimated number of Canada geese within BPHS strata predominantly occupied by these geese (strata 1-6, 8, 10-12) in 2004 decreased 29% from 2003 levels. These estimates have declined an average of 2% per year since 1995 (P=0.123). Throughout most of Alaska, spring phenology was early and spring flooding was limited. Nesting success of lesser Canada geese in the interior was assessed as good and production should be above average. Spring snowmelt on the North Slope was delayed slightly but geese appeared to initiate nests earlier than average. Production of these geese should be above average.

Aleutian *Canada* *Geese* *(ACG):* These geese now nest primarily on the Aleutian Islands, although historically they nested from near Kodiak Island, Alaska to the Kuril Islands in Asia. They now winter along the Pacific Coast to central California (Fig. 3). The Aleutian Canada goose was listed as endangered in 1967 (the population numbered approximately 800 birds in 1974) and was delisted in 2001.

An indirect population estimate based on observations of neckbanded geese in California during 2003-2004 was 69,900 (± 11,600), 12% higher than last year's record high (P=0.459, Fig. 18). These indirect estimates have increased an average of 12% per year over the last 10 years (P<0.001). The Aleutian Islands experienced low winter snowfall and an early spring breakup and green-up. A survey crew on Nizki Island in 2004 found more than 4 times more nests than were found in 1998. Aleutian geese there nested earlier in 2004 than previously recorded, which should lead to good production.

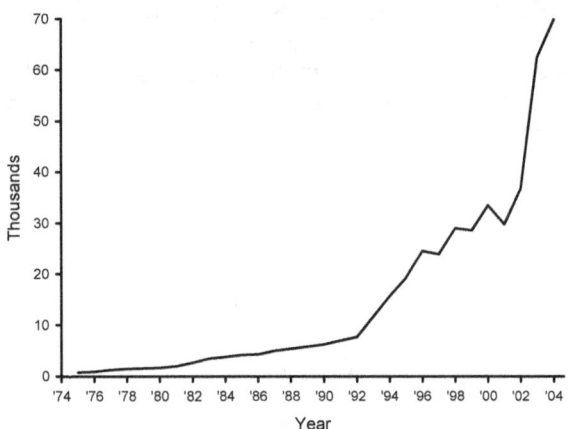

Fig. 18. Number of Aleutian Canada geese estimated from winter estimates and mark-resight methods.

Status of Light Geese

The term light geese refers to both snow geese and Ross's geese (including both white and blue color phases), and the lesser (*C. c. caerulescens*) and greater (*C. c. atlantica*) snow goose subspecies. Another collective term, mid-continent light geese, includes lesser snow and Ross's geese of 2 populations: the Mid-continent Population and the Western Central Flyway Population.

Ross's *Geese:* Most Ross's geese nest in the Queen Maud Gulf region, but increasing numbers nest along the western coast of Hudson Bay and Southampton, Baffin, and Banks Islands. Ross's geese are present in the range of 3 different populations of light geese and primarily winter in California, New Mexico, Texas, and Mexico, with increasing numbers in Louisiana and Arkansas (Fig. 19).

Periodic photo-inventories and annual surveys in the Queen Maud Gulf indicate the spring Ross's goose population has increased rapidly and has exceeded 800,000 geese in recent years. Annual estimates of total population size in winter are not available, but surveys on wintering areas of light geese indicate increases in range, number, and proportions of Ross's geese. The largest Ross's goose colony is near Karrak Lake in the Queen Maud Gulf. Researchers estimated that 433,800 adult Ross's geese nested there in 2003, a 19% increase from 2002 (Fig. 20). These estimates have increased an average of 11% per year from 1995-2003 (P<0.001). Spring snowmelt was earlier than average near Queen Maud Gulf but goose arrival was delayed, apparently by the persistent snow cover in a broad strip from the Mackenzie River mouth to the Hudson Bay coast. Nest initiation at

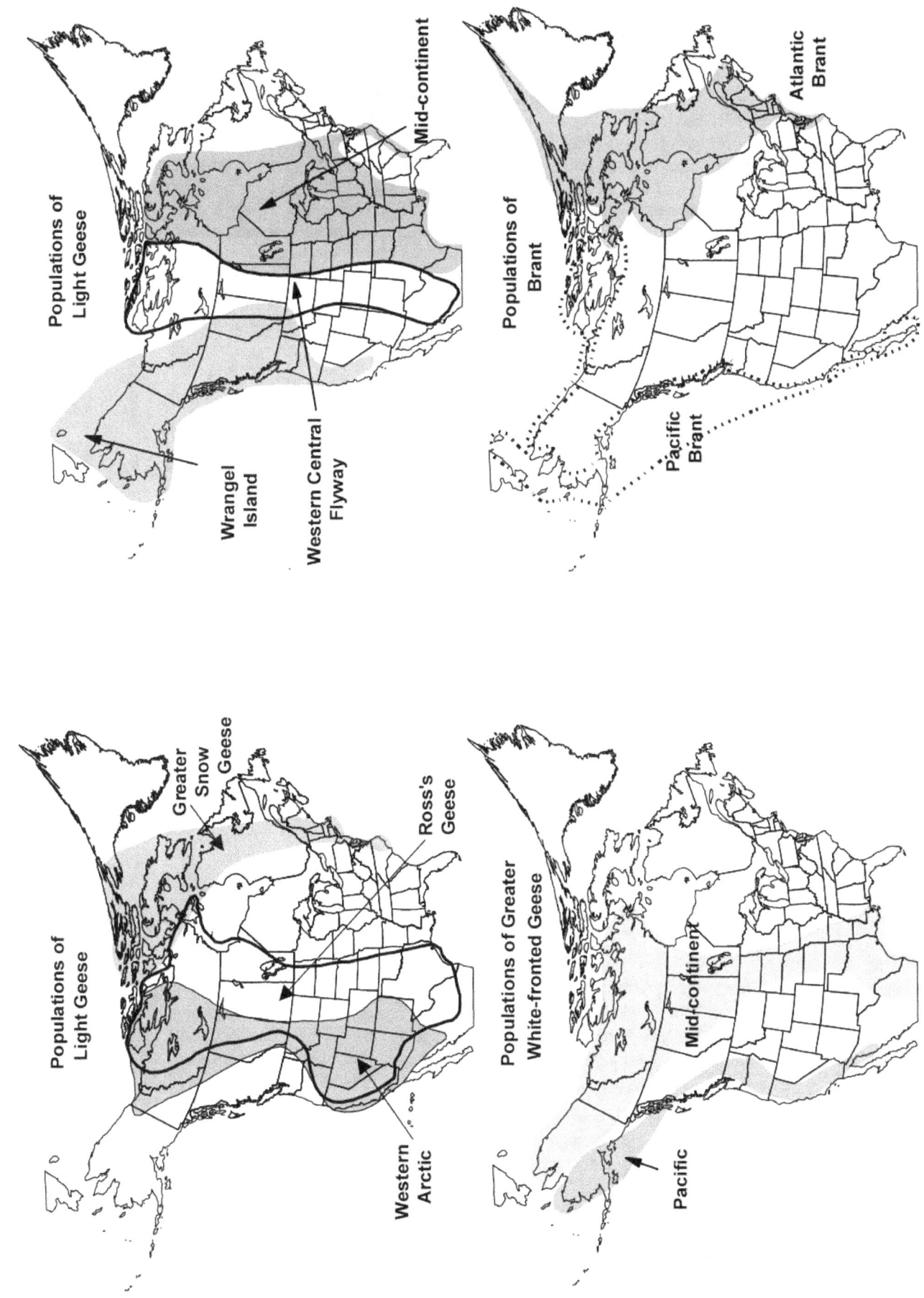

Fig. 19. Approximate ranges of brant and snow, Ross's, and white-fronted goose populations in North America.

Karrak Lake in 2004 was about 8 days later than average and clutch sizes were reduced from the long-term mean. Weather conditions during the incubation period were generally unfavorable. Increasing numbers of Ross's geese are nesting near the McConnell River, where nest initiation was delayed by about 3 weeks compared to 2003. Nest success there was poor in 2004. Under similar circumstances of near-average spring phenology on major light goose breeding areas and broad areas of snow cover in migration habitats in 2002, harvest age ratios for Ross's geese were depressed considerably. Conditions in 2004 were similar to those in 2002, but nesting conditions at McConnell River and incubation weather in the Queen Maud Gulf were harsher this year. Overall, Ross's geese are expected to experience below average production this year. The size of the fall flight cannot be predicted without an annual index to the size of the total breeding population.

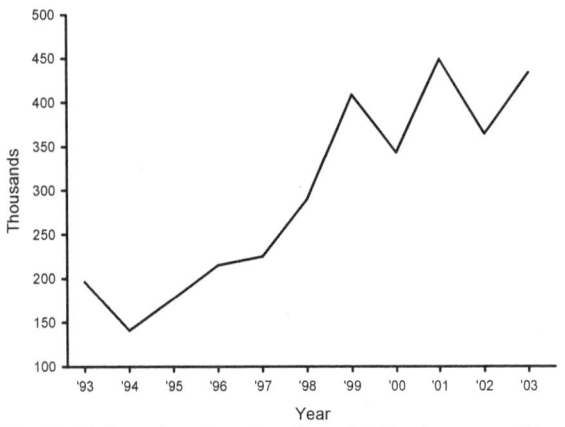

Fig. 20. Estimated number of nesting adult Ross's geese at Karrak Lake Colony, Nunavut.

Mid-continent Population Light Geese (MCP): This population, including lesser snow geese and increasing numbers of Ross's geese, nests along the west coast of Hudson Bay and on Southampton and Baffin Islands (Fig. 19). These geese winter primarily in eastern Texas, Louisiana, and Arkansas.

During the 2004 MWS, biologists counted 2,154,100 light geese, 12% fewer than last year (Fig. 21, a portion of Louisiana was not surveyed in 2004). Due to declines in these indices since 1997, the 1995-2004 data now indicate an average decline of 2% per year (P=0.087). Biologists on Southampton and Baffin Islands during June reported snow and ice conditions similar to, or slightly delayed from last year. However, goose arrival and nest initiation might have been delayed by persistent snow cover on migration areas near Hudson Bay. Under similar

conditions in 2002, harvest age ratios for light geese were depressed substantially. Clutch sizes from a small sample of snow goose nests on Baffin Island were slightly reduced from those observed in 2003. Survey biologists' impressions were that nesting effort on Southampton Island was reduced from 2003. High nest destruction rates were reported from 3 Hudson Bay Colonies. At La Perouse Bay, spring phenology was extremely late in 2004. Biologists there suggest the late nesting phenology and natural senescence of food plants with fall photo-period will yield poor survival of late hatched goslings. The production and fall flight of MCP geese likely will be reduced from 2003 levels when nesting conditions were favorable.

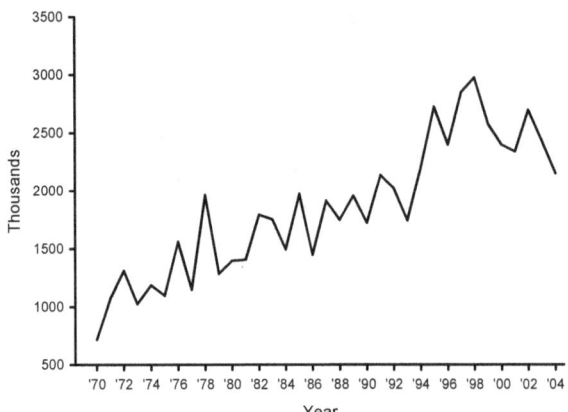

Fig. 21. Estimated number of Mid-continent Population light geese (lesser snow and Ross's geese) during winter.

Western Central Flyway Population (WCFP): This population is composed primarily of snow geese but includes a substantial proportion of Ross's geese. WCF geese nest in the central and western Canadian Arctic, with large nesting colonies near the Queen Maud Gulf and on Banks Island. These geese stage during fall in eastern Alberta and western Saskatchewan and concentrate during winter in southeastern Colorado, New Mexico, the Texas Panhandle, and the northern highlands of Mexico (Fig. 19).

WCFP geese wintering in the U.S. portion of their range are surveyed annually, but the entire range, including Mexico, is surveyed only once every 3 years. In the U.S. portion of the survey, 135,300 geese were counted in January 2004, 28% more than last year (Fig. 22). There has been no trend in growth for this population during 1995-2004 (P=0.783). Spring snowmelt was earlier than average near Queen Maud Gulf but goose arrival was delayed, apparently by the persistent snow cover in a broad strip from the Mackenzie River mouth to the Hudson Bay coast. A BPHS survey crew in southern Saskatchewan observed relatively high numbers of geese in May 2004, which may have reflected a suspended northward migration. Nest initiation at Karrak Lake in 2004 was about 8 days later than average and clutch sizes were reduced from the long-term mean. Under the circumstance of near-average spring phenology on major light goose breeding areas and broad areas of snow cover in migration habitats in 2002, harvest age ratios for light geese were depressed considerably. Weather conditions during the incubation period were generally unfavorable for geese in the Queen Maud Gulf. Spring phenology on Banks Island was reported as late, and Inuvialuit residents reported a reduced nesting effort there. Overall, production is expected to be below average for this population.

River or Kendall Island in 2004. At Wrangel Island's Tundra River colony, nesting phenology was near average. Preliminary estimates from biologists on Wrangel Island include a spring population of 110,000, >28,000 nests, a mean clutch size of 3.6 eggs, and 75% nest success. These estimates are consistent with above average production. A fall flight similar to last year's is expected.

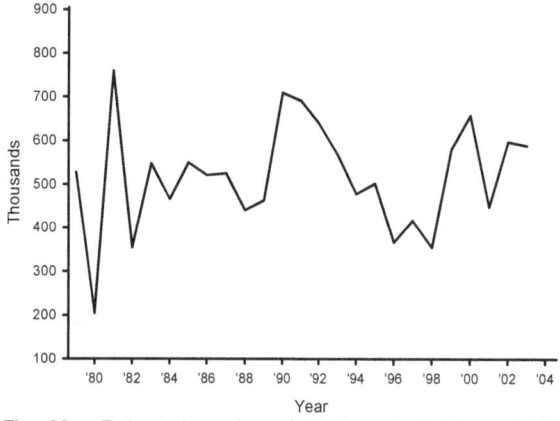

Fig. 23. Estimated number of Western Arctic/Wrangel Island Population light geese during fall.

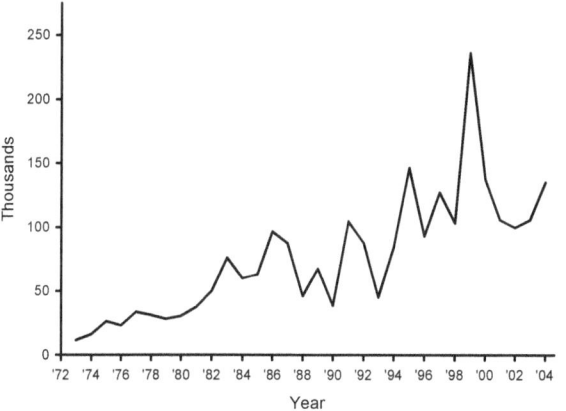

Fig. 22. Estimated number of Western Central Flyway Population light geese during winter in the United States.

Western Arctic/Wrangel Island Population (WAWI): Most of the snow geese in the Pacific Flyway originate from nesting colonies in the western and central Arctic (WA: Banks Island, the Anderson and Mackenzie River Deltas, the western Queen Maud Gulf region) or Wrangel Island (WI), located off the northern coast of Russia. The WA segment of the population winters in central and southern California, New Mexico, and Mexico; the WI segment winters in the Puget Sound area of Washington and in northern and central California (Fig. 19). In winter, WA and WI segments commingle with light geese from other populations in California, complicating winter surveys.

The fall 2003 estimate of WAWI snow geese was 587,800, 2% lower than estimated in 2002 (Fig. 23). Fall estimates have increased 4% per year during 1994-2003 (*P*=0.132). Spring phenology on Banks Island was reported as late, and Inuvialuit residents reported a reduced nesting effort there. Surveys indicated little nesting effort at Andersen

Greater Snow Geese (GSG): This subspecies principally nests on Bylot, Axel Heiberg, Ellesmere, and Baffin Islands, and on Greenland. These geese winter along the Atlantic coast from New Jersey to North Carolina (Fig. 19).

This population is monitored on their spring staging areas near the St. Lawrence Valley in Quebec. Using improved methodology (use of 5 survey aircraft rather than 3) the preliminary estimate from spring 2004 was 957,600 (± 81,100), 41% higher than the last year's final estimate (678,000, Fig. 24). Spring estimates of greater snow geese have increased an average of 2% per year since 1995 (*P*=0.155). The number of snow geese counted during the 2004 MWS in the Atlantic Flyway was 552,100, a 37% increase from the previous survey. Midwinter counts have increased an average of 5% per year during 1995-2004 (*P*=0.059). The largest known greater snow goose nesting colony is on Bylot Island. There, initial snowmelt and nesting effort occurred earlier than average but a week of cold and snow interrupted and prolonged the nest initiation period. Overall, nesting effort will be reduced from the high level in 2003. Despite high nest success, near average clutch sizes, and good weather during the hatching period, biologists expected only average production. A fall flight similar to last year's is expected.

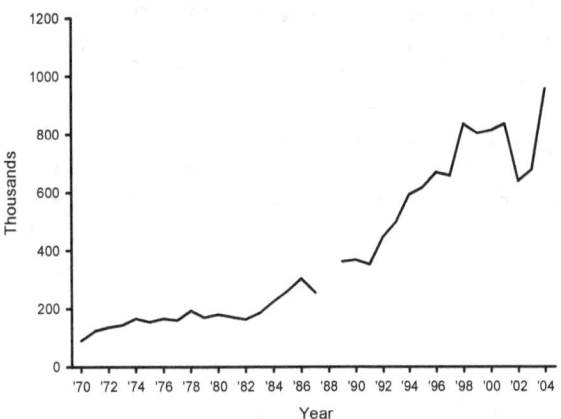

Fig. 24. Estimated number of greater snow geese during spring.

Status of Greater White-fronted Geese

Pacific Population White-fronted Geese (PP): These geese primarily nest on the Yukon Delta of Alaska and winter in the Central Valley of California (Fig. 19).

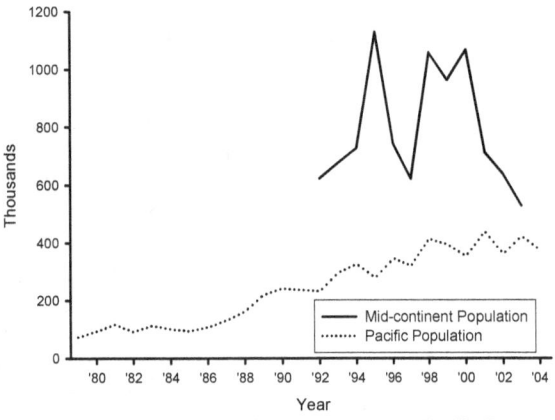

Fig. 25. Estimated number of Mid-continent and Pacific Population greater white-fronted geese during fall.

The index for this population was a fall estimate from 1979-1998. Since 1999, the index has been a fall population estimate derived from spring surveys of adults on the Yukon-Kuskokwim Delta (YKD) and Bristol Bay. The 2004 fall estimate is 374,900, 11% lower than in 2003 (Fig. 25). These estimates have increased an average of 3% per year since 1995 (*P*=0.049). Spring aerial surveys in the YKD coastal zone indicated decreases in total white-fronts (15%) and breeding pairs (7%) from 2003 levels. Spring estimates of total white-fronted geese on the entire YKD and Bristol Bay have increased an average of 2% per year from 1995-2004 (*P*=0.122). An early spring snowmelt led to advanced nesting phenology in 2004. The number of nests found during YKD nesting surveys in 2004 was the highest recorded

since 1982. Clutch sizes and nest success were also above average. A fall flight similar to last year's is expected.

Mid-continent Population White-fronted Geese (MCP): These white-fronted geese nest across a broad region from central and northwestern Alaska to the central Arctic and the Foxe Basin. They concentrate in southern Saskatchewan during the fall and in Texas, Louisiana, and Mexico during winter (Fig. 19).

During the fall 2003 survey in Saskatchewan and Alberta, biologists counted 528,200 MCP geese, a decrease of 17% from the 2002 count (Fig. 25). During 1994-2003, these estimates have declined an average of 3% per year (*P*=0.270). Spring phenology in MCP range varied from early in Alaska's interior to late in the western Canadian Arctic. In the Queen Maud Gulf region spring phenology was earlier than average but goose arrival may have been delayed by the persistent snow cover in a broad strip from the Mackenzie River mouth to the Hudson Bay coast. On Alaska's North Slope white-fronted goose broods were observed earlier than average. Production of white-fronted geese in 2004 was assessed as above average in interior Alaska, likely near average or slightly below near Queen Maud Gulf and Victoria Island, and below average in the western Canadian Arctic. A fall flight somewhat lower than last year's is expected.

Status of Brant

Atlantic Brant (ATLB): Most of this population nests on islands of the eastern Arctic. These brant winter along the Atlantic Coast from Massachusetts to North Carolina (Fig. 19).

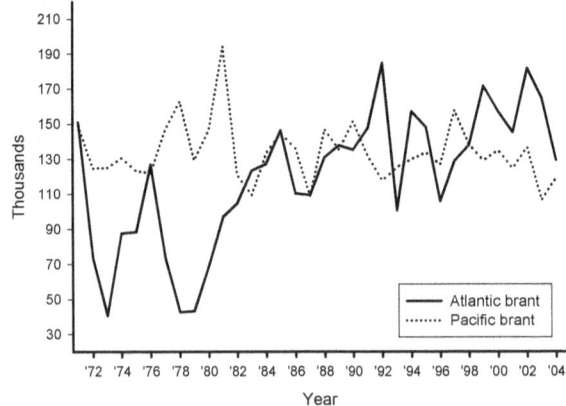

Fig. 26. Estimated number of Atlantic and Pacific Population brant during winter.

The 2004 MWS estimate of brant in the Atlantic Flyway was 129,600, 21% fewer than last year's estimate (Fig. 26). These estimates have increased an average of 2% per year for the most recent 10-year period (P=0.227). Biologists on Southampton and Baffin Islands during June reported snow and ice conditions similar to or slightly delayed from 2003. However, brant arrival to nesting areas may have been delayed by persistent snow cover on migration areas near Hudson and James Bays in 2004. Under similar conditions in 2002, harvest age ratios for brant were depressed substantially.

Pacific Brant (PACB): These brant nest across Alaska's Yukon-Kuskokwim Delta (YKD) and North Slope, Banks Island, other islands of the western and central Arctic, the Queen Maud Gulf, and Wrangel Island. They winter as far south as Baja California and the west coast of Mexico (Fig. 19).

The 2004 MWS in the Pacific Flyway and Mexico resulted in a count of 119,200 brant, 12% more than the previous year's count (Fig. 26). These estimates have decreased an average of 2% per year during 1995-2004 (P=0.081). Spring phenology was early on the YKD, slightly delayed on the North Slope, and delayed on Banks and other northern islands. Brant nesting effort in 2004 increased in 4 of the 5 colonies on the YKD from 2004, but remained approximately 24% below the 8-year average. Clutch sizes and nest success on the YKD were higher than in the very poor year of 2003. Production of brant in 2004 should be improved somewhat over 2003, but the fall flight is expected to be similar to last year's.

Western High Arctic Brant (WHA): This recently recognized population of brant nests on the Parry Islands of the Northwest Territories. The population stages in fall at Izembek Lagoon, Alaska. They predominantly winter in Padilla, Samish, and Fidalgo Bays of Washington and near Boundary Bay, British Columbia, although some individuals have been observed as far south as Mexico. The development of a management plan and monitoring program are underway for this newly designated population.

According to satellite imagery, most of Melville and Prince Patrick Islands remained snow covered on 30 June 2004. This suggests another poor production year for WHA brant.

Status of Emperor Geese

The breeding range of emperor geese is restricted to coastal areas of the Bering Sea, with the largest concentration on the Yukon-Kuskokwim Delta (YKD) in Alaska. Emperor geese migrate relatively short distances and primarily winter in the Aleutian Islands (Fig. 27). Since 1981, emperor geese have been surveyed annually on spring staging areas in southwestern Alaska.

The spring 2004 emperor survey estimate was 47,400 geese, 34% lower than last year (Fig. 28). These estimates have shown no trend for the last 10-year period (P=0.829). Spring indices of breeding pairs from the YKD coastal survey increased 19%, and the total bird index was unchanged from 2003 levels. An early spring snowmelt led to advanced emperor goose nesting phenology in 2004, the earliest in 20 years. YKD nesting surveys indicated record-high nest numbers, and higher than average nest success and mean clutch size. A fall flight larger than last year's is expected.

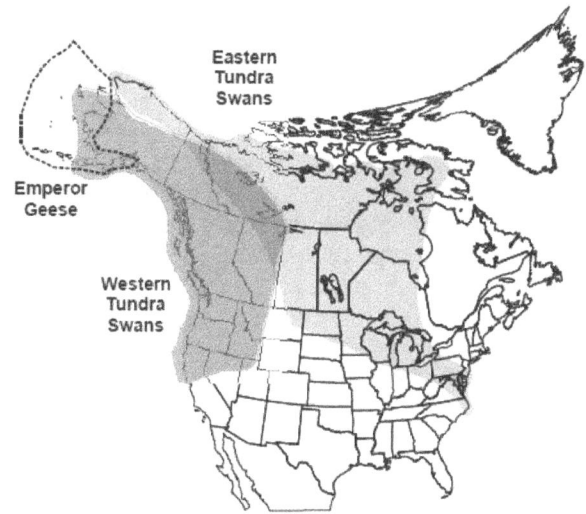

Fig. 27. Approximate range of emperor geese, and eastern and western tundra swan populations in North America.

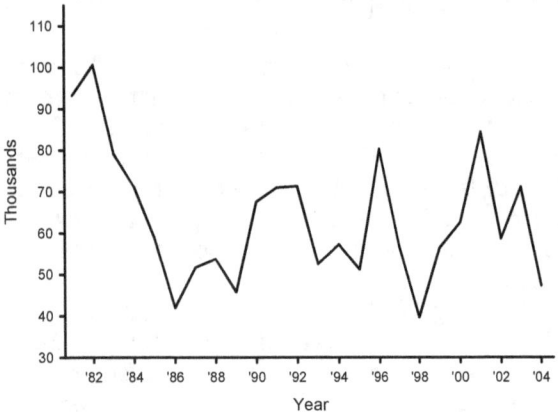

Fig. 28. Estimated numbers of emperor geese present during May surveys.

Status of Tundra Swans

Western Population Tundra Swans: These swans nest along the coastal lowlands of western Alaska, particularly between the Yukon and Kuskokwim Rivers. They winter primarily in California, Utah, and the Pacific Northwest (Fig. 27).

The 2004 MWS estimate of 83,000 swans was 19% lower than the 2003 estimate (Fig. 29). These estimates have shown no trend for the last 10 years (P=0.851). Spring phenology was very early throughout most of western Alaska. Surveys in the coastal zone of the YKD during spring 2004 indicated breeding swan and total swan numbers increased 20% and 18% from 2003, respectively. Nest plot surveys indicated an increase in swan nests from 2003, a record-high clutch size (5.5 eggs) and above average nest success. A fall flight larger than last year's is expected.

Eastern Population Tundra Swans: Eastern Population tundra swans nest from the Seward Peninsula of Alaska to the northeast shore of Hudson Bay and Baffin Island. These birds winter in coastal areas from Maryland to North Carolina (Fig. 27)

During the 2004 MWS, 95,000 eastern tundra swans were observed, 12% fewer than last year (Fig. 29). During the last 10 years, these estimates have increased an average of 3% per year (P=0.018). Spring phenology on the mainland of the western Canadian Arctic was delayed and breeding success there will likely be reduced. Nesting conditions in most other major breeding areas were near average or slightly delayed (less important breeding areas around Hudson Bay were greatly delayed) but swan reproductive success also may have been reduced by harsh conditions on migration habitats in 2004. Overall, a fall flight lower that last year's is expected.

Fig. 29. Estimated numbers of Eastern and Western Population tundra swans during winter.

Appendix A. Individuals that supplied information on the status of ducks.

Alaska, Yukon Territory, and Old Crow Flats (Strata 1-12): B. Conant and D. Groves

Northern Alberta, Northeastern British Columbia, and Northwest Territories (Strata 13-18, 20, and 77): C. Ferguson and W. Mullins

Northern Saskatchewan and Northern Manitoba (Strata 21-24): F. Roetker and P. Stinson

Southern and Central Alberta (Strata 26-29, 75, and 76):
Air	E. Buelna Huggins and C. Pyle
Ground	P. Pryor[a], K. Froggatt[b], S. Barry[a], E. Hofman[b], C. Procter[a], M. Barr[c], N. Clements[a], N. Fontaine[c], J. Going[a], R. Hunka[c], T. Mathews[c], B. Peers[c], R. Russell[b], J. Spenst[c], and K. Zimmer[a]

Southern Saskatchewan (Strata 30-35):
Air	P. Thorpe, T. Lewis, R. King, and C. Reighn
Ground	D. Nieman[a], J. Smith[a], K. Warner[a], K. Dufour[a], C. Wilkinson[a], K. Cochrane[a], P. Nieman[a], A. Williams[c], M. Schuster[a], D. Caswell[a], J. Leafloor[a], P. Rakowski[a], F. Baldwin[a], R. Bazin[a], J. Caswell[a], J. Galbraith[a], C. Lindgren[c], C. Meuckon[a], and N. Wiebe[a]

Southern Manitoba (Strata 25 and 36-40):
Air	R. King and C. Reighn
Ground	M. Schuster[a], D. Caswell[a], J. Leafloor[a], P. Rakowski[a], F. Baldwin[a], G. Ball[b], J. Caswell[a], J. Ga braith[a], C. Lindgren[c], C. Meuckon[a], N. Wiebe[a], and R. Olson[d]

Montana and Western Dakotas (Strata 41-44):
Air	J. Voelzer and R. Bentley
Ground	K. Richkus and D. D'Auria

Eastern Dakotas (Strata 45-49):
Air	J. Solberg and M. Rich
Ground	P. Garrettson, A. Araya, K. Kruse, and T. Thorn

Central Quebec (Strata 68 and 69):
Air	J. Wortham, D. Fronczak, and J. Goldsberry[d]
Helicopter	D. Holtby[b], R. Raftovich, and G. Boomer

New York, Eastern Ontario, and Southern Quebec (Strata 52-56): M. Koneff, D. Forsell, and M. Jones

Central and Western Ontario (Strata 50 and 51): K. Bollinger and W. Butler

Maine and Maritimes (Strata 62-67): J. Bidwell and M. Drut

British Columbia: A. Breault[b], P. Watts[d], and participants from the Canadian Wildlife Service, Ducks Unlimited Canada, British Columbia Wildlife Branch, Canadian Parks Service, and private organizations

California:
Air	D. Yparraguirre[b] and M. Weaver[b]
Ground	D. Loughman[d] and J. Laughlin[d]

Colorado: J. Gammonley[b]

Michigan: S. Chadwick[b], B. Dybas-Berger[b], E. Flegler[b], E. Kafcas[b], A. Karr[b], J. Niewoonder[b], T. Oliver[b], J. Robison[b], B. Scullon[b], and V. Weigold[b]

Minnesota:
Air	A. Buchert[b] and S. Cordts[b]
Ground	S. Kelly, J. Artmann, W. Brininger, J. Holler, R. Papasso, T. Rondeau, S. Zodrow, K. Bosquet, L. Deede, C. Hanson, D. Johnson, J. Kelley, A. Rife, and L. Wolff

Nebraska:
Air	D. Benning[d] M. Vrtiska[b], and N. Lyman[d]
Ground	T. Krol kowski[b]
Data Analysis	M. Vrtiska[b]

Nevada: C. Mortimore[b] and N. Saake[b]

Appendix A. Continued.

Northeastern U.S.:
Data Analysis	B. Raftovich and H. Bellary
Connecticut	M. Huang [b] K. Kubik [b], and K. LeRose [b]
Delaware	T. Whittendale [b]
Maryland	unavailable
Massachusetts	Massachusetts Division of Fisheries and Wildlife personnel
New Hampshire	E. Robinson [b], J. Robinson [b], E. Orff [b], T. Walski [b], K. Bordeau [b], K. Bontaites [b], W. Staats [b], W. Ingham [b], J. Kelley [b], W. Staats [b], K. Tuttle [b], A.Timmins [b], and S. Wheeler [b]
New Jersey	T. Nichols [b], J. Garris [b], C. Gruber [b], B. Kirkpatrick [b], J. Mangino [b], J. Powers [b], L. Widjeskog [b], D. Wilkinson [b], J. Ziemba [b], and N. Zimpfer [b]
New York	Staff and volunteers of the NY State Department of Environmental Conservation
Pennsylvania	M. Casalena [b], J. Dunn [b], J. Gilbert [b], I. Gregg [b], T. Hardisty [b], K. Jacobs [b], A. Keister [b], M. Lovallo [b], B. Palmer [b], C. Rosenbery [b], M. Ternent [b], and C. Thoma [b]
Rhode Island	C. Brown [b], L. G bson [b], T. Silvia [d], and B. Tefft [b]
Vermont	D. Sausville [b], T. Appleton [b], J. Austin [b], J. Buck [b], D. Blodgett [b], F. Hammond [b], J. Mlcuch [b], and K. Royar [b]
Virginia	unavailable

Oregon:
Air	B. Bales, B. Brim [d], B. Bowen [d], M. St. Louis [b], T. Collom [b], and M. Kirsch [b]
Data Analysis	S. Nelson [b], B. Bales [b], and A. Turacek [d]

Washington: R. Friesz [b], D. Base [b], D. Volsen [b], H. Ferguson [b], P. Fowler [b], J. Tabor [b], J. Cotton [b], T. McCall [b], B. Patterson [b], S. Fitkin [b], J. Heinlen [b], M. Livingston [b], J. Bernatowicz [b], E. Krausz [b], and T. Hames [b]

Wisconsin:
Air	B. Bacon [b], C. Cold [b], C. Milestone [b], and B. Glenzinski [b]
Ground	K. Van Horn [b], T. Bahti [b], K. Belling [b], N. Christel [b], J. Cole [b], P. David [b], G. Dunsmoor [b], B. Hill [b], J. Huff [b], R. Lichtie [b], D. Matheys [b], R. McDonough [b], K. Morgan [b], A. Nelson [b], D. North [b], A. Oberc, [b] J. Robaidek [b], M. Windsor [b], A. Kitchen, R. Krueger, L. Nieman, J. Ruwaldt, and G. VanVreede,

Wyoming: L. Roberts [b]

We also wish to acknowledge the following individuals and groups:
The states of the Atlantic and Mississippi Flyway and Regions 3, 4, and 5 of the U.S. Fish and Wildlife Service for collecting mid-winter waterfowl survey data, from which we extract black duck counts, and J. Serie, K. Gamble, B. Raftovich, and D. Fronczak for summarizing the counts; and the volunteers of the North American Breeding Bird Survey (a survey coordinated by the U.S. Geological Survey, Biological Resources Division [USGS/BRD]) for data used in estimation of wood duck population trends, and J. Sauer, USGS for conducting the wood duck trend analyses.

---

[a] Canadian Wildlife Service
[b] State, Provincial, or Tribal Conservation Agency
[c] Ducks Unlimited - Canada
[d] Other organization
All others – U.S. Fish and Wildlife Service

Appendix B. Individuals that supplied information on the status of geese and swans.

Flyway-wide and Regional Survey Reports: T. Bowman, D. Caswell[a], K. Dickson[a], M. Drut, J. Fischer, D. Fronczak, K. Gamble, K. Kruse, R. Oates, R. Raftovich, J. Serie, D. Sharp, R. Stehn, R. Trost, and G. Walters

Information from the Breeding Population and Habitat Survey: see Appendix A

North Atlantic Population of Canada Geese: J. Bidwell and M. Bateman[a]

Atlantic Population of Canada Geese: R. Cotter[a], J. Dunn[b], W. Harvey[a], L. Hindman[b], P. May[d], J. Rodrigue[a], and A. Tulugak[d]

Atlantic Flyway Resident Population of Canada Geese: P. Castelli[b], G. Chasko[b], G. Costanzo[b], J. Dunn[b], L. Garland[b], L. Gibson[b], H. Heusmann[b], L. Hindman[b], M. Huang[b], K. Jacobs[b], W. Lesser[b], R. Raftovich, E. Robinson[b], T. Whittendale[b], and S. Wilson[b]

Southern James Bay Population of Canada Geese: K. Abraham[b], J. Hughes[a], K. Ross[a], and L. Walton[b]

Mississippi Valley Population of Canada Geese: K. Abraham[b], J. Bergquist[b], J. Hughes[a], A. Jano[b], K. Ross[a], and L. Walton[b]

Mississippi Flyway Population Giant Canada Geese: K. Abraham[b], K. Chodachek[b], D. Graber[b], M. Gillespie[b], R. Helm[b], J. Hughes[a], J. Lawrence[b], D. Luukkonen[b], R. Marshalla[b], R. Pritchert[b], M. Shieldcastle[b], K. Van Horn[b], E. Warr[b], and G. Zenner[b]

Eastern Prairie Population of Canada Geese: D. Andersen[d], M. Gillespie[b], B. Lubinski, A. Raedeke[b], and P. Telander[b]

Western Prairie and Great Plains Populations of Canada Geese: M. Johnson[b], M. Kraft[b], D. Nieman[a], M. O'Meilia[b], P. Thorpe, S. Vaa[b], M. Vritiska[b]

Tall Grass Prairie Population of Canada Geese: J. Caswell[a], V. Johnston[a], J. Leafloor[a], B. Lubinski, M. Mallory[a], and K. Warner[a]

Short Grass Prairie Population of Canada Geese: R. Alisauskas[a], C. Ferguson, K. Kruse, and J. Hines[a]

Hi-Line Population of Canada Geese: J. Dubovsky, J. Gammonley[b], J. Hansen[b], D. Nieman[a], and L. Roberts[b]

Rocky Mountain Population of Canada Geese: T. Aldrich[b], J. Bohne[b], J. Dubovsky, J. Herbert[b], T. Hinz[b], C. Mortimore[b], L. Roberts[b], T. Sanders[b], and P. Thorpe

Pacific Population of Canada Geese: A. Breault[a], B. Bales[b], C. Feldheim[b], C. Ferguson, T. Hemker[b], T. Hinz[b], D. Kraege[b], C. Mortimore[b], M. Weaver, and D. Yparraguirre[b]

Dusky Canada Geese: M. Drut, B. Eldridge, T. Fondell, B. Larned, D. Logan[d], D. Robertson, and T. Rothe[b]

Lesser and Taverner's Canada Geese: B. Conant, E. Mallek, and M. Spindler

Cackling Canada Geese: M. Anthony[d], C. Dau, B. Eldridge, D. Marks, B. Platte, and M. Wege

Aleutian Canada Geese: V. Byrd and J. Williams

Greater Snow Geese: D. Bordage[a], G. Gauthier[d], J. Giroux[d], J. Lefebvre[a], M. Mallory[a], A. Reed[a], and E. Reed

Mid-continent Population Light Geese: K. Abraham[b], B. Andres, J. Caswell[d], M. Gillespie[b], B. Lubinski, A. Raedeke[b], V. Johnston[a], J. Leafloor[a], M. Mallory[a], R. Rockwell[d], K. Ross[a], P. Telander[b], and L. Walton[b]

Western Central Flyway Population Light Geese: R. Alisauskas[a], J. Hines[a], K. Kruse, and P. Thorpe

Appendix B. Continued.

Western Arctic/Wrangel Island Population of Lesser Snow Geese: V. Baranuk[d], S. Boyd[a], J. Hines[a], and D. Kraege[b]

Ross's Geese: R. Alisauskas[a], J. Caswell[d], J. Leafloor[a], and P. Thorpe

Pacific Population White-Fronted Geese: C. Dau, B. Eldridge, C. Ely[d], D. Groves, D. Marks, and B. Platte

Mid-continent Population White-fronted Geese: R. Alisauskas[a], B. Conant, J. Hines[a], B. Larned, K. Lehmkuhl, E. Malleck, D. Nieman[a], B. Scotton, M. Spindler, and K. Warner[a]

Pacific Brant: M. Anthony[d], B. Eldridge, and R. King

Atlantic Brant: G. Gilchrist, M. Mallory[a], A. Reed[a], and M. Robertson

Western High Arctic Brant: D. Kraege[b]

Emperor Geese: C. Dau, B. Eldridge, R. King, E. Malleck, D. Marks, and B. Platte

Western Population of Tundra Swans: C. Dau and B. Eldridge

Eastern Population of Tundra Swans: C. Dau, J. Hines[a], and B. Larned

---

[a]Canadian Wildlife Service
[b]State, Provincial, or Tribal Conservation Agency
[c]Ducks Unlimited - Canada
[d]Other organization
All others - U.S. Fish and Wildlife Service

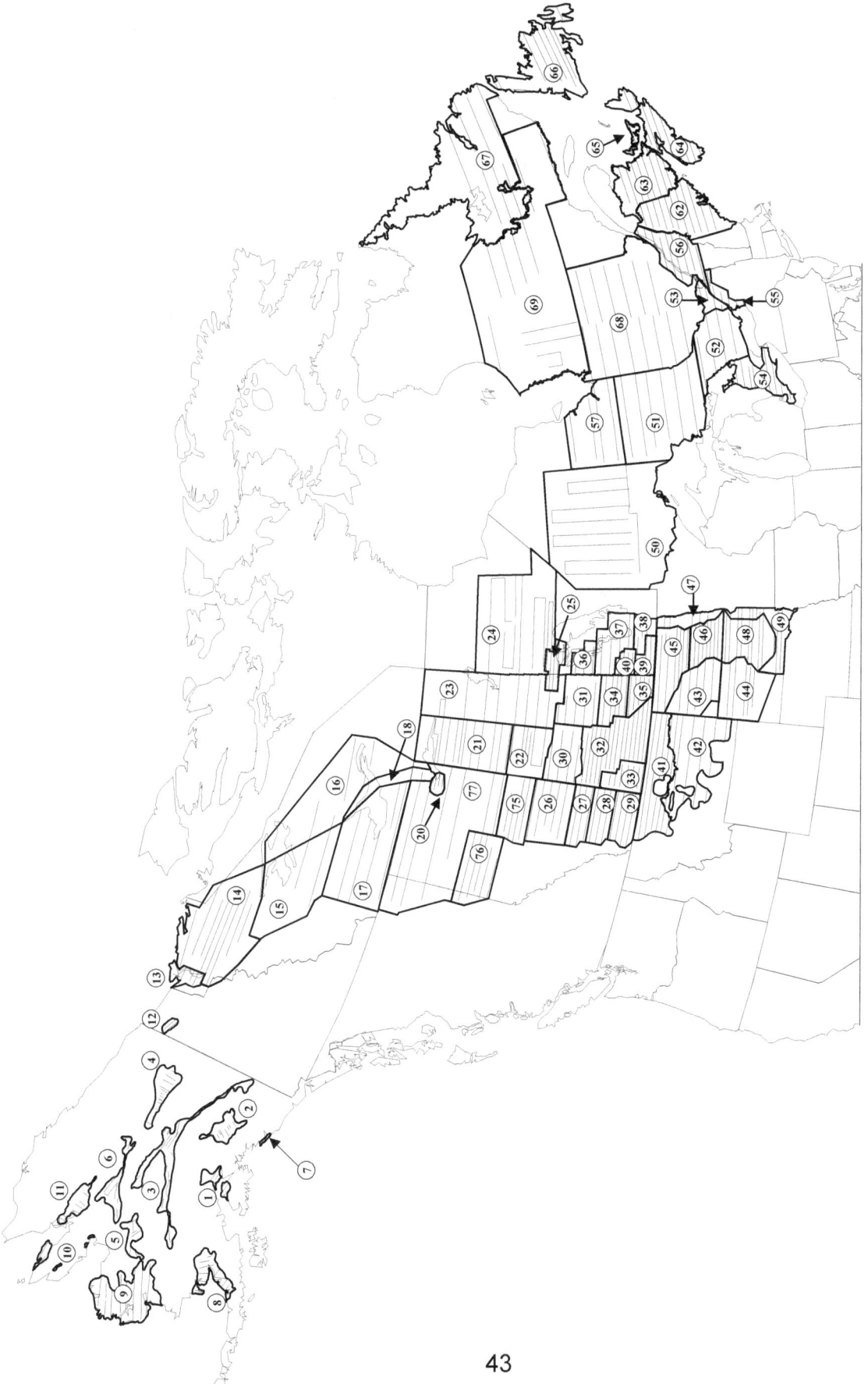

Appendix C. Strata and transects for areas of the May Waterfowl Breeding Population and Habitat Survey (stratum 57 is experimental and survey counts are not included in this report).

Appendix D. Estimated number of May ponds and standard errors (in thousands) in portions of Prairie Canada and the northcentral U.S.

Year	Prairie Canada		Northcentral U.S. [a]		Total	
	$\hat{N}$	$\hat{SE}$	$\hat{N}$	$\hat{SE}$	$\hat{N}$	$\hat{SE}$
1961	1977.2	165.4				
1962	2369.1	184.6				
1963	2482.0	129.3				
1964	3370.7	173.0				
1965	4378.8	212.2				
1966	4554.5	229.3				
1967	4691.2	272.1				
1968	1985.7	120.2				
1969	3547.6	221.9				
1970	4875.0	251.2				
1971	4053.4	200.4				
1972	4009.2	250.9				
1973	2949.5	197.6				
1974	6390.1	308.3	1840.8	197.2	8230.9	366.0
1975	5320.1	271.3	1910.8	116.1	7230.9	295.1
1976	4598.8	197.1	1391.5	99.2	5990.3	220.7
1977	2277.9	120.7	771.1	51.1	3049.1	131.1
1978	3622.1	158.0	1590.4	81.7	5212.4	177.9
1979	4858.9	252.0	1522.2	70.9	6381.1	261.8
1980	2140.9	107.7	761.4	35.8	2902.3	113.5
1981	1443.0	75.3	682.8	34.0	2125.8	82.6
1982	3184.9	178.6	1458.0	86.4	4642.8	198.4
1983	3905.7	208.2	1259.2	68.7	5164.9	219.2
1984	2473.1	196.6	1766.2	90.8	4239.3	216.5
1985	4283.1	244.1	1326.9	74.0	5610.0	255.1
1986	4024.7	174.4	1734.8	74.4	5759.5	189.6
1987	2523.7	131.0	1347.8	46.8	3871.5	139.1
1988	2110.1	132.4	790.7	39.4	2900.8	138.1
1989	1692.7	89.1	1289.9	61.7	2982.7	108.4
1990	2817.3	138.3	691.2	45.9	3508.5	145.7
1991	2493.9	110.2	706.1	33.6	3200.0	115.2
1992	2783.9	141.6	825.0	30.8	3608.9	144.9
1993	2261.1	94.0	1350.6	57.1	3611.7	110.0
1994	3769.1	173.9	2215.6	88.8	5984.8	195.3
1995	3892.5	223.8	2442.9	106.8	6335.4	248.0
1996	5002.6	184.9	2479.7	135.3	7482.2	229.1
1997	5061.0	180.3	2397.2	94.4	7458.2	203.5
1998	2521.7	133.8	2065.3	89.2	4586.9	160.8
1999	3862.0	157.2	2842.3	256.8	6704.3	301.1
2000	2422.2	96.1	1524.5	99.9	3946.9	138.6
2001	2747.2	115.6	1893.2	91.5	4640.4	147.4
2002	1439.0	105.0	1281.1	63.4	2720.0	122.7
2003	3522.3	151.8	1667.8	67.4	5707.1	168.7
2004	2512.6	131.0	1407.0	101.7	3912.0	165.8

[a] No comparable survey data available for the northcentral U.S. during 1961-73.

Appendix E. Breeding population estimates (in thousands) for total ducks[a] and mallards for states, provinces, or regions that conduct spring surveys.

Year	British Columbia[b] Total Ducks	Mallards	California Total Ducks	Mallards	Colorado Total Ducks	Mallards	Michigan Total Ducks	Mallards	Minnesota Total Ducks	Mallards	Nebraska Total Ducks	Mallards
1955	[c]										101.5	32.0
1956											94.9	25.8
1957											154.8	26.8
1958											176.4	28.1
1959											99.7	12.1
1960					51.1	32.4					143.6	21.6
1961					58.7	32.4					141.8	43.3
1962					72.7	59.4					68.9	35.8
1963					78.0	62.1					114.9	37.4
1964					110.8	64.0					124.8	66.8
1965					111.9	60.2					52.9	20.8
1966					100.8	57.8					118.8	36.0
1967					122.2	69.7					96.2	27.6
1968					145.4	73.3			368.5	83.7	96.5	24.1
1969					138.1	57.5			345.3	88.8	100.6	26.7
1970					114.8	46.5			343.8	113.9	112.4	24.5
1971					121.4	48.3			286.9	78.5	96.0	22.3
1972					94.6	45.0			237.6	62.2	91.7	15.2
1973					112.3	45.2			415.6	99.8	85.5	19.0
1974					129.0	56.9			332.8	72.8	67.4	19.5
1975					156.7	38.2			503.3	175.8	62.6	14.8
1976					142.0	34.6			759.4	117.8	87.2	20.1
1977									536.6	134.2	152.4	24.1
1978					145.1	42.6			511.3	146.8	126.0	29.0
1979					103.2	30.9			901.4	158.7	143.8	33.6
1980					110.7	32.0			740.7	172.0	133.4	37.3
1981					188.4	36.4			515.2	154.8	66.2	19.4
1982					70.2	30.1			558.4	120.5	73.2	22.3
1983					130.6	44.2			394.2	155.8	141.6	32.2
1984					109.9	39.3			563.8	188.1	154.1	36.1
1985									580.3	216.9	75.4	28.4
1986					105.0	42.0			537.5	233.6	69.5	15.1
1987					125.4	62.0			614.9	192.3	120.5	41.7
1988	6.0	0.6			123.1	63.4			752.8	271.7	126.5	27.8
1989	5.5	0.5			122.9	48.2			1021.6	273.0	136.7	18.7
1990	5.9	0.6			131.9	56.5			886.8	232.1	81.4	14.7
1991	7.4	0.7			124.1	49.8			868.2	225.0	126.3	26.0
1992	7.7	0.7	497.4	375.8	101.3	46.6	665.8	384.0	1127.3	360.9	63.4	24.4
1993	7.1	0.6	666.7	359.0	145.6	68.7	813.5	454.3	875.9	305.8	92.8	23.8
1994	7.8	0.6	483.2	311.7	141.3	68.9	848.3	440.6	1320.1	426.5	118.9	17.5
1995	8.7	0.9	589.7	368.5	123.5	54.5	812.6	559.8	912.2	319.4	142.9	42.0
1996	8.3	0.6	843.7	536.7	142.8	60.1	790.2	395.8	1062.4	314.8	132.3	38.9
1997	8.1	0.6	824.3	511.3	107.5	51.9	886.3	489.3	953.0	407.4	128.3	26.1
1998	9.2	1.1	706.8	353.9	89.1	44.8	1305.2	567.1	739.6	368.5	155.7	43.4
1999	8.3	0.8	851.0	560.1	101.0	50.2	824.8	494.3	716.5	316.4	251.2[d]	81.1
2000	7.8	0.6	562.4	347.6			1121.7	462.8	815.3	318.1	178.8	54.3
2001	7.4	0.6	413.5	302.2	26.5[e]	11.8	673.5	358.2	761.3	320.6	225.3	69.2
2002	8.6	0.5	392.0	265.3			997.3	336.8	1224.1	366.6	141.8	50.6
2003	8.2	0.5	533.7	337.1			587.2	294.1	748.9	280.5	96.7	32.9
2004	6.3	0.5	412.8	262.4			701.9	328.8	1099.3	375.3	69.9	23.2

[a] Species composition for the total duck estimate varies by region.
[b] Index to waterfowl use in prime waterfowl producing areas of the province.
[c] Blanks denote that the survey was not conducted, results were not available, or survey methods changed.
[d] First year of survey after major changes in survey methodology. Hence, results from earlier years are not comparable.

Appendix E. Continued.

Year	Nevada Total Ducks	Nevada Mallards	Northeastern US[e] Total Ducks	Northeastern US[e] Mallards	Oregon Total Ducks	Oregon Mallards	Washington Total Ducks	Washington Mallards	Wisconsin Total Ducks	Wisconsin Mallards
1955										
1956										
1957										
1958										
1959	14.2	2.1								
1960	14.1	2.1								
1961	13.5	2.0								
1962	13.8	1.7								
1963	23.8	2.2								
1964	23.5	3.0								
1965	29.3	3.5								
1966	25.7	3.4								
1967	11.4	1.5								
1968	10.5	1.2								
1969	18.2	1.4								
1970	19.6	1.5								
1971	18.3	1.1								
1972	19.0	0.9								
1973	20.7	0.7							412.7[f]	107.0
1974	17.1	0.7							435.2	94.3
1975	14.5	0.6							426.9	120.5
1976	13.6	0.6							379.5	109.9
1977	16.5	1.0							323.3	91.7
1978	11.1	0.6							271.3	61.6
1979	12.8	0.6					98.6	32.1	265.7	78.6
1980	16.6	0.9					113.7	34.1	248.1	116.5
1981	26.9	1.6					148.3	41.8	505.0	142.8
1982	21.0	1.1					146.4	49.8	218.7	89.5
1983	24.3	1.5					149.5	47.6	202.3	119.5
1984	24.0	1.4					196.3	59.3	210.0	104.8
1985	24.9	1.5					216.2	63.1	192.8	73.9
1986	26.4	1.3					203.8	60.8	262.0	110.8
1987	33.4	1.5					183.6	58.3	389.8	136.9
1988	31.7	1.3					241.8	67.2	287.1	148.9
1989	18.8	1.3	1144.8	589.9			162.3	49.8	462.5	180.7
1990	22.2	1.3	1042.3	665.1			168.9	56.9	328.6	151.4
1991	14.6	1.4	1849.2	779.2			140.8	43.7	435.8	172.4
1992	12.4	0.9	1090.2	562.2			116.3	41.0	683.8	249.7
1993	14.1	1.2	1198.4	683.1			149.8	55.0	379.4	174.5
1994	19.2	1.4	1348.1	853.1	396.8	160.9	123.9	52.7	571.2	283.4
1995	17.9	1.0	1441.2	862.8	278.7	104.5	147.3	58.9	592.4	242.2
1996	26.4	1.7	1432.3	848.5	348.9	124.3	163.3	61.6	536.3	314.4
1997	25.3	2.5	1404.9	795.1	458.8	144.2	172.8	67.0	409.3	181.0
1998	27.9	2.1	1443.8	775.1	391.7	142.1	185.3	79.0	412.8	186.9
1999	29.9	2.3	1520.8	879.7	363.8	144.3	200.2	86.2	476.6	248.4
2000	26.1	2.1	1925.8	757.8	366.3	121.7	143.6	47.7	744.4	454.0
2001	22.2	2.0	1392.6	807.5			146.4	50.5	440.1	183.5
2002	11.7	0.7	1465.7	833.3	303.9	116.8	133.3	44.7	740.8	378.5
2003	21.1	1.7	1303.7	731.8	298.2	109.9	127.8	39.8	533.5	261.3
2004	24.2	1.7	1417.9	809.1	301.1	102.8	114.9	40.0	651.5	229.2

[e] Includes all or portions of Connecticut, Delaware, Maryland, Massachusetts, New Hampshire, New Jersey, New York, Pennsylvania, Rhode Island, Vermont, and Virginia.
[f] Survey estimates do not match those from previous reports because they have been recalculated.

46

Appendix F. Breeding population estimates and standard errors (in thousands) for 10 species of ducks from the traditional survey area (strata 1-18, 20-50, 75-77).

	Mallard		Gadwall		American wigeon		Green-winged teal		Blue-winged teal	
Year	$\hat{N}$	$\hat{SE}$	$\hat{N}$	$\hat{SE}$	$\hat{N}$	$\hat{SE}$	$\hat{N}$	$\hat{SE}$	$\hat{N}$	$\hat{SE}$
1955	8777.3	457.1	651.5	149.5	3216.8	297.8	1807.2	291.5	5305.2	567.6
1956	10452.7	461.8	772.6	142.4	3145.0	227.8	1525.3	236.2	4997.6	527.6
1957	9296.9	443.5	666.8	148.2	2919.8	291.5	1102.9	161.2	4299.5	467.3
1958	11234.2	555.6	502.0	89.6	2551.7	177.9	1347.4	212.2	5456.6	483.7
1959	9024.3	466.6	590.0	72.7	3787.7	339.2	2653.4	459.3	5099.3	332.7
1960	7371.7	354.1	784.1	68.4	2987.6	407.0	1426.9	311.0	4293.0	294.3
1961	7330.0	510.5	654.8	77.5	3048.3	319.9	1729.3	251.5	3655.3	298.7
1962	5535.9	426.9	905.1	87.0	1958.7	145.4	722.9	117.6	3011.1	209.8
1963	6748.8	326.8	1055.3	89.5	1830.8	169.9	1242.3	226.9	3723.6	323.0
1964	6063.9	385.3	873.4	73.7	2589.6	259.7	1561.3	244.7	4020.6	320.4
1965	5131.7	274.8	1260.3	114.8	2301.1	189.4	1282.0	151.0	3594.5	270.4
1966	6731.9	311.4	1680.4	132.4	2318.4	139.2	1617.3	173.6	3733.2	233.6
1967	7509.5	338.2	1384.6	97.8	2325.5	136.2	1593.7	165.7	4491.5	305.7
1968	7089.2	340.8	1949.0	213.9	2298.6	156.1	1430.9	146.6	3462.5	389.1
1969	7531.6	280.2	1573.4	100.2	2941.4	168.6	1491.0	103.5	4138.6	239.5
1970	9985.9	617.2	1608.1	123.5	3469.9	318.5	2182.5	137.7	4861.8	372.3
1971	9416.4	459.5	1605.6	123.0	3272.9	186.2	1889.3	132.9	4610.2	322.8
1972	9265.5	363.9	1622.9	120.1	3200.1	194.1	1948.2	185.8	4278.5	230.5
1973	8079.2	377.5	1245.6	90.3	2877.9	197.4	1949.2	131.9	3332.5	220.3
1974	6880.2	351.8	1592.4	128.2	2672.0	159.3	1864.5	131.2	4976.2	394.6
1975	7726.9	344.1	1643.9	109.0	2778.3	192.0	1664.8	148.1	5885.4	337.4
1976	7933.6	337.4	1244.8	85.7	2505.2	152.7	1547.5	134.0	4744.7	294.5
1977	7397.1	381.8	1299.0	126.4	2575.1	185.9	1285.8	87.9	4462.8	328.4
1978	7425.0	307.0	1558.0	92.2	3282.4	208.0	2174.2	219.1	4498.6	293.3
1979	7883.4	327.0	1757.9	121.0	3106.5	198.2	2071.7	198.5	4875.9	297.6
1980	7706.5	307.2	1392.9	98.8	3595.5	213.2	2049.9	140.7	4895.1	295.6
1981	6409.7	308.4	1395.4	120.0	2946.0	173.0	1910.5	141.7	3720.6	242.1
1982	6408.5	302.2	1633.8	126.2	2458.7	167.3	1535.7	140.2	3657.6	203.7
1983	6456.0	286.9	1519.2	144.3	2636.2	181.4	1875.0	148.0	3366.5	197.2
1984	5415.3	258.4	1515.0	125.0	3002.2	174.2	1408.2	91.5	3979.3	267.6
1985	4960.9	234.7	1303.0	98.2	2050.7	143.7	1475.4	100.3	3502.4	246.3
1986	6124.2	241.6	1547.1	107.5	1736.5	109.9	1674.9	136.1	4478.8	237.1
1987	5789.8	217.9	1305.6	97.1	2012.5	134.3	2006.2	180.4	3528.7	220.2
1988	6369.3	310.3	1349.9	121.1	2211.1	139.1	2060.8	188.3	4011.1	290.4
1989	5645.4	244.1	1414.6	106.6	1972.9	106.0	1841.7	166.4	3125.3	229.8
1990	5452.4	238.6	1672.1	135.8	1860.1	108.3	1789.5	172.7	2776.4	178.7
1991	5444.6	205.6	1583.7	111.8	2254.0	139.5	1557.8	111.3	3763.7	270.8
1992	5976.1	241.0	2032.8	143.4	2208.4	131.9	1773.1	123.7	4333.1	263.2
1993	5708.3	208.9	1755.2	107.9	2053.0	109.3	1694.5	112.7	3192.9	205.6
1994	6980.1	282.8	2318.3	145.2	2382.2	130.3	2108.4	152.2	4616.2	259.2
1995	8269.4	287.5	2835.7	187.5	2614.5	136.3	2300.6	140.3	5140.0	253.3
1996	7941.3	262.9	2984.0	152.5	2271.7	125.4	2499.5	153.4	6407.4	353.9
1997	9939.7	308.5	3897.2	264.9	3117.6	161.6	2506.6	142.5	6124.3	330.7
1998	9640.4	301.6	3742.2	205.6	2857.7	145.3	2087.3	138.9	6398.8	332.3
1999	10805.7	344.5	3235.5	163.8	2920.1	185.5	2631.0	174.6	7149.5	364.5
2000	9470.2	290.2	3158.4	200.7	2733.1	138.8	3193.5	200.1	7431.4	425.0
2001	7904.0	226.9	2679.2	136.1	2493.5	149.6	2508.7	156.4	5757.0	288.8
2002	7503.7	246.5	2235.4	135.4	2334.4	137.9	2333.5	143.8	4206.5	227.9
2003	7949.7	267.3	2549.0	169.9	2551.4	156.9	2678.5	199.7	5518.2	312.7
2004	7425.3	282.0	2589.6	165.6	1981.3	114.9	2460.8	145.2	4073.0	238.0

Year	Northern shoveler $\hat{N}$	$\hat{SE}$	Northern pintail $\hat{N}$	$\hat{SE}$	Redhead $\hat{N}$	$\hat{SE}$	Canvasback $\hat{N}$	$\hat{SE}$	Scaup $\hat{N}$	$\hat{SE}$
1955	1642.8	218.7	9775.1	656.1	539.9	98.9	589.3	87.8	5620.1	582.1
1956	1781.4	196.4	10372.8	694.4	757.3	119.3	698.5	93.3	5994.1	434.0
1957	1476.1	181.8	6606.9	493.4	509.1	95.7	626.1	94.7	5766.9	411.7
1958	1383.8	185.1	6037.9	447.9	457.1	66.2	746.8	96.1	5350.4	355.1
1959	1577.6	301.1	5872.7	371.6	498.8	55.5	488.7	50.6	7037.6	492.3
1960	1824.5	130.1	5722.2	323.2	497.8	67.0	605.7	82.4	4868.6	362.5
1961	1383.0	166.5	4218.2	496.2	323.3	38.8	435.3	65.7	5380.0	442.2
1962	1269.0	113.9	3623.5	243.1	507.5	60.0	360.2	43.8	5286.1	426.4
1963	1398.4	143.8	3846.0	255.6	413.4	61.9	506.2	74.9	5438.4	357.9
1964	1718.3	240.3	3291.2	239.4	528.1	67.3	643.6	126.9	5131.8	386.1
1965	1423.7	114.1	3591.9	221.9	599.3	77.7	522.1	52.8	4640.0	411.2
1966	2147.0	163.9	4811.9	265.6	713.1	77.6	663.1	78.0	4439.2	356.2
1967	2314.7	154.6	5277.7	341.9	735.7	79.0	502.6	45.4	4927.7	456.1
1968	1684.5	176.8	3489.4	244.6	499.4	53.6	563.7	101.3	4412.7	351.8
1969	2156.8	117.2	5903.9	296.2	633.2	53.6	503.5	53.7	5139.8	378.5
1970	2230.4	117.4	6392.0	396.7	622.3	64.3	580.1	90.4	5662.5	391.4
1971	2011.4	122.7	5847.2	368.1	534.4	57.0	450.7	55.2	5143.3	333.8
1972	2466.5	182.8	6979.0	364.5	550.9	49.4	425.9	46.0	7997.0	718.0
1973	1619.0	112.2	4356.2	267.0	500.8	57.7	620.5	89.1	6257.4	523.1
1974	2011.3	129.9	6598.2	345.8	626.3	70.8	512.8	56.8	5780.5	409.8
1975	1980.8	106.7	5900.4	267.3	831.9	93.5	595.1	56.1	6460.0	486.0
1976	1748.1	106.9	5475.6	299.2	665.9	66.3	614.4	70.1	5818.7	348.7
1977	1451.8	82.1	3926.1	246.8	634.0	79.9	664.0	74.9	6260.2	362.8
1978	1975.3	115.6	5108.2	267.8	724.6	62.2	373.2	41.5	5984.4	403.0
1979	2406.5	135.6	5376.1	274.4	697.5	63.8	582.0	59.8	7657.9	548.6
1980	1908.2	119.9	4508.1	228.6	728.4	116.7	734.6	83.8	6381.7	421.2
1981	2333.6	177.4	3479.5	260.5	594.9	62.0	620.8	59.1	5990.9	414.2
1982	2147.6	121.7	3708.8	226.6	616.9	74.2	513.3	50.9	5532.0	380.9
1983	1875.7	105.3	3510.6	178.1	711.9	83.3	526.6	58.9	7173.8	494.9
1984	1618.2	91.9	2964.8	166.8	671.3	72.0	530.1	60.1	7024.3	484.7
1985	1702.1	125.7	2515.5	143.0	578.2	67.1	375.9	42.9	5098.0	333.1
1986	2128.2	112.0	2739.7	152.1	559.6	60.5	438.3	41.5	5235.3	355.5
1987	1950.2	118.4	2628.3	159.4	502.4	54.9	450.1	77.9	4862.7	303.8
1988	1680.9	210.4	2005.5	164.0	441.9	66.2	435.0	40.2	4671.4	309.5
1989	1538.3	95.9	2111.9	181.3	510.7	58.5	477.4	48.4	4342.1	291.3
1990	1759.3	118.6	2256.6	183.3	480.9	48.2	539.3	60.3	4293.1	264.9
1991	1716.2	104.6	1803.4	131.3	445.6	42.1	491.2	66.4	5254.9	364.9
1992	1954.4	132.1	2098.1	161.0	595.6	69.7	481.5	97.3	4639.2	291.9
1993	2046.5	114.3	2053.4	124.2	485.4	53.1	472.1	67.6	4080.1	249.4
1994	2912.0	141.4	2972.3	188.0	653.5	66.7	525.6	71.1	4529.0	253.6
1995	2854.9	150.3	2757.9	177.6	888.5	90.6	770.6	92.2	4446.4	277.6
1996	3449.0	165.7	2735.9	147.5	834.2	83.1	848.5	118.3	4217.4	234.5
1997	4120.4	194.0	3558.0	194.2	918.3	77.2	688.8	57.2	4112.3	224.2
1998	3183.2	156.5	2520.6	136.8	1005.1	122.9	685.9	63.8	3471.9	191.2
1999	3889.5	202.1	3057.9	230.5	973.4	69.5	716.0	79.1	4411.7	227.9
2000	3520.7	197.9	2907.6	170.5	926.3	78.1	706.8	81.0	4026.3	205.3
2001	3313.5	166.8	3296.0	266.6	712.0	70.2	579.8	52.7	3694.0	214.9
2002	2318.2	125.6	1789.7	125.2	564.8	69.0	486.6	43.8	3524.1	210.3
2003	3619.6	221.4	2558.2	174.8	636.8	56.6	557.6	48.0	3734.4	225.5
2004	2810.4	163.9	2184.6	155.2	605.3	51.5	617.2	64.6	3807.2	202.3

Appendix G. Total breeding duck estimates for the traditional and eastern survey areas in thousands.

Year	Traditional survey area [a]		Eastern survey area [b]	
	$\hat{N}$	$\hat{SE}$	$\hat{N}$	$\hat{SE}$
1955	39603.6	1264.0		
1956	42035.2	1177.3		
1957	34197.1	1016.6		
1958	36528.1	1013.6		
1959	40089.9	1103.6		
1960	32080.5	876.8		
1961	29829.0	1009.0		
1962	25038.9	740.6		
1963	27609.5	736.6		
1964	27768.8	827.5		
1965	25903.1	694.4		
1966	30574.2	689.5		
1967	32688.6	796.1		
1968	28971.2	789.4		
1969	33760.9	674.6		
1970	39676.3	1008.1		
1971	36905.1	821.8		
1972	40748.0	987.1		
1973	32573.9	805.3		
1974	35422.5	819.5		
1975	37792.8	836.2		
1976	34342.3	707.8		
1977	32049.0	743.8		
1978	35505.6	745.4		
1979	38622.0	843.4		
1980	36224.4	737.9		
1981	32267.3	734.9		
1982	30784.0	678.8		
1983	32635.2	725.8		
1984	31004.9	716.5		
1985	25638.3	574.9		
1986	29092.8	609.3		
1987	27412.1	562.1		
1988	27361.7	660.8		
1989	25112.8	555.4		
1990	25079.2	539.9	1057.8	108.6
1991	26605.6	588.7	1105.9	116.4
1992	29417.9	605.6	1346.9	112.2
1993	26312.4	493.9	1330.1	254.0
1994	32523.5	598.2	1272.3	126.6
1995	35869.6	629.4	1269.2	127.1
1996	37753.0	779.6	3665.2	372.3
1997	42556.3	718.9	2337.8	196.6
1998	39081.9	652.0	2953.5	194.5
1999	43435.8	733.9	3213.7	216.8
2000	41838.3	740.2	3204.1	345.7
2001	36177.5	633.1	3336.7	252.0
2002	31181.1	547.8	4398.6	303.5
2003	36225.1	664.7	3635.3	281.7
2004	32164.0	579.8	3905.3	329.8

[a] Total ducks in the traditional survey area include species in Appx. G plus black duck, ring-necked duck, goldeneyes, bufflehead, and ruddy duck.
[b] Species in the East includes those in Appx. H plus gadwall, northern shoveler, northern pintail, and scaup.

Appendix H. Breeding population estimates and standard errors (in thousands) for the 10 most abundant species of ducks in the eastern survey area, 1990-2004 [a].

Year	Mergansers $\hat{N}$	$\hat{SE}$	Mallard $\hat{N}$	$\hat{SE}$	American black duck $\hat{N}$	$\hat{SE}$	American wigeon $\hat{N}$	$\hat{SE}$	Am. green-winged teal $\hat{N}$	$\hat{SE}$	Lesser scaup $\hat{N}$	$\hat{SE}$	Ring-necked duck $\hat{N}$	$\hat{SE}$	Goldeneyes $\hat{N}$	$\hat{SE}$	Bufflehead $\hat{N}$	$\hat{SE}$	Scoters $\hat{N}$	$\hat{SE}$
1990	157.5	48.3	208.6	47.7	160.9	33.5	31.0	22.6	47.1	8.6	135.7	56.2	92.1	28.3	73.3	22.2	99.9	22.9	1.9	1.9
1991	263.9	78.6	169.8	34.5	126.0	35.3	45.4	21.8	42.2	14.4	43.5	16.4	158.1	30.2	138.4	44.3	94.1	32.1	6.4	5.3
1992	128.1	24.3	362.2	54.1	160.3	33.1	15.4	9.3	43.8	13.9	65.6	23.2	251.6	62.3	241.0	55.2	59.0	13.7	3.0	2.3
1993	164.9	23.7	333.8	49.7	124.6	25.6	9.4	7.4	47.4	9.9	288.6	235.3	248.1	65.1	90.2	32.6	13.1	3.6	0.0	0.0
1994	358.4	91.8	238.6	28.8	116.3	20.7	18.9	9.6	169.2	24.0	81.9	31.7	163.5	62.6	55.0	17.4	33.4	14.0	18.3	9.7
1995	376.3	89.7	212.6	41.1	234.5	46.6	13.8	7.9	96.2	14.1	62.0	20.5	195.6	51.0	9.2	3.7	26.5	8.8	5.0	4.8
1996	1083.1	279.6	387.6	63.6	562.2	97.1	34.7	17.0	436.2	86.9	38.5	15.1	611.9	98.7	410.3	169.7	50.6	12.5	23.6	10.5
1997	379.1	53.0	287.6	44.8	434.5	63.1	22.5	11.2	211.5	31.3	16.7	7.2	617.6	151.1	220.6	54.8	22.3	6.7	88.9	50.2
1998	327.4	38.8	363.2	71.3	542.1	55.4	83.6	24.6	299.5	81.1	20.1	10.6	361.8	53.8	715.7	124.7	44.6	10.3	159.4	47.1
1999	290.0	39.4	280.8	39.2	488.7	51.3	121.1	45.6	422.4	62.3	44.9	20.5	453.2	76.0	920.0	167.3	70.5	20.8	47.0	17.7
2000	400.0	54.0	212.3	31.3	396.9	53.9	41.7	20.4	201.6	28.7	19.8	9.1	618.8	71.3	946.5	318.7	49.3	11.3	182.1	59.0
2001	428.7	62.8	285.7	40.8	422.0	48.8	77.5	18.2	220.3	33.5	203.5	92.2	352.8	39.6	1032.2	202.4	95.0	20.9	178.6	49.4
2002	815.2	97.9	295.1	38.1	602.8	86.1	86.6	25.5	604.1	129.0	136.1	48.2	416.0	57.8	954.9	209.2	83.6	21.2	314.4	76.4
2003	569.1	63.9	383.1	57.8	532.6	60.2	79.0	32.8	452.3	120.1	101.2	21.2	399.3	50.3	767.9	212.1	66.3	17.0	237.1	66.9
2004	668.0	110.5	367.9	58.2	729.8	154.3	27.0	11.0	553.8	125.1	81.1	35.7	667.6	152.6	429.9	147.4	43.8	11.1	260.9	81.5

[a] Maine estimates were included beginning in 1995. Quebec estimates were included beginning in 1996. Therefore, estimates are only comparable within year groups 1990-94, and 1996-present.

Appendix I. Estimated number of July ponds and standard errors (in thousands) in portions of Prairie Canada and the northcentral U.S.

Year	Prairie Canada $\hat{N}$	Prairie Canada $\hat{SE}$	Northcentral U.S.[a] $\hat{N}$	Northcentral U.S.[a] $\hat{SE}$	Total $\hat{N}$	Total $\hat{SE}$
1961	562.0	50.9				
1962	738.2	60.9				
1963	1813.2	98.7				
1964	1308.3	60.0				
1965	2231.0	113.9				
1966	1979.2	111.7				
1967	1498.4	94.5				
1968	802.9	50.7				
1969	1658.6	90.6				
1970	2613.3	143.9				
1971	2016.7	112.2				
1972	1312.5	77.8				
1973	1735.5	146.8				
1974	2753.2	136.1	609.6	45.1	3362.8	143.4
1975	2410.1	121.1	922.8	51.6	3332.9	131.7
1976	2137.6	101.6	786.8	46.8	2924.4	111.8
1977	1391.2	74.1	469.4	38.6	1860.6	83.6
1978	1520.3	63.5	697.1	41.4	2217.4	75.8
1979	1803.0	88.7	754.6	38.5	2557.6	96.7
1980	898.8	52.0	336.1	14.3	1234.9	53.9
1981	873.0	43.6	457.6	22.7	1330.6	49.2
1982	1662.0	85.9	882.2	50.3	2544.2	99.5
1983	2264.1	108.8	957.9	51.7	3222.0	120.4
1984	1270.3	90.1	1270.6	67.1	2540.9	112.4
1985	1563.1	91.2	753.5	39.3	2316.5	99.3
1986	1610.0	71.4	1056.9	46.1	2666.9	85.0
1987	1225.7	69.2	858.0	31.0	2083.7	75.8
1988	1009.2	63.8	518.7	26.4	1527.9	69.0
1989	932.4	47.9	731.3	32.8	1663.7	58.0
1990	1297.6	70.5	663.2	42.0	1960.7	82.1
1991	2562.8	127.2	865.0	40.9	3427.8	133.7
1992	1272.4	55.9	664.2	24.8	1936.8	61.2
1993	2292.5	102.6	1384.8	65.4	3677.4	121.7
1994	2329.9	105.7	1079.7	43.2	3409.6	114.2
1995	1773.4	95.3	1576.5	69.6	3350.0	118.0
1996	2648.2	94.2	1218.2	64.9	3866.4	114.3
1997	2489.7	96.5	1347.1	54.1	3836.8	110.6
1998	2850.7	149.0	1353.3	56.8	4203.9	159.5
1999	2047.1	124.3	1036.7	73.8	3083.8	144.6
2000	2450.8	95.9	1401.5	82.1	3852.4	126.3
2001	1837.9	73.0	1031.7	56.5	2869.7	92.3
2002	996.7	118.7	839.6	43.5	1836.3	126.5
2003	1465.5	63.8	1018.4	39.4	2483.8	75.0
2004	[b]	.	.	.	.	.

[a] No comparable survey data available for the northcenral U.S. during 1961-73.
[b] Surveys not flown.

51

Appendix J. Population indices (in thousands) for North American Canada goose populations, 1969-2004.

Year	North Atlantic[a,b]	Atlantic[a,b]	Atlantic Flyway Resident[a]	Southern James Bay[a]	Miss. Valley[a]	Miss. Flyway Giant[a]	Eastern Prairie[a]	W. Prairie & Great Plains[c]	Tall Grass Prairie[c,g]	Short Grass Prairie[d]	Hi-line[d]	Rocky Mountain[d]	Dusky[d]	Cackling[e]	Aleutian[h]
1969/70										151.2	44.2	25.8	22.5		
1970/71									131.1	148.5	40.5	25.4	19.8		
1971/72							124.7		159.6	160.9	31.4	36.7	17.9		
1972/73							137.6		147.2	259.4	35.6	37.2	15.8		
1973/74							119.9		158.5	153.6	24.5	43.0	18.6		
1974/75							144.4		125.6	123.7	41.2	46.9	26.5		0.8
1975/76							216.5		201.5	242.5	55.6	51.7	23.0		0.9
1976/77							163.8		167.9	210.0	67.6	54.8	24.1		1.3
1977/78							179.7		211.3	134.0	65.1	59.4	24.0		1.5
1978/79							99.4		180.5	163.7	33.8	64.6	25.5	64.1	1.6
1979/80									155.2	213.0	67.3	75.9	22.0	127.4	1.7
1980/81							125.5		244.9	168.2	94.4	93.2	23.0	87.1	2.0
1981/82							131.8	175.0	268.6	156.0	81.9	64.7	17.7	54.1	2.7
1982/83							155.1	242.0	165.5	173.2	75.9	71.4	17.0	26.2	3.5
1983/84							135.6	150.0	260.7	143.5	39.5	62.6	10.1	25.8	3.8
1984/85							158.4	230.0	197.3	179.1	76.4	92.4	7.5	32.1	4.2
1985/86							194.8	115.0	189.4	181.0	69.8	71.7	12.2	51.4	4.3
1986/87							203.2	324.0	159.0	190.9	98.1	75.3		54.8	5.0
1987/88		118.0					209.2	272.1	306.1	139.1	66.8	75.7	12.2	69.9	5.4
1988/89			396.0		657.8		210.2	330.3	213.0	284.8	100.1	92.3	11.8	76.8	5.8
1989/90			236.6	82.4	825.0		231.8	271.0	146.5	378.1	105.9	135.1	11.7	110.2	6.3
1990/91			305.7	108.1	620.3		211.8	390.0	305.1	508.5	116.6	98.4		104.6	7.0
1991/92			439.2	91.6	782.3		202.5	341.9	276.3	620.2	140.5	134.1	18.0	149.3	7.7
1992/93		91.3	647.4	77.3	547.1	810.9	157.5	318.0	235.3	328.2	118.5	91.9	16.7	164.3	11.7
1993/94		40.1	648.3	95.7	741.2	1002.9	210.8	272.5	224.2	434.1	164.3	90.9	11.0	152.5	15.7
1994/95		29.3	780.0	94.0	796.2	1030.6	204.6	352.5	245.0	697.8	174.4	120.2	8.5	161.4	19.2
1995/96	99.6	46.1	932.6	123.0	593.9	1132.4	190.4	403.3	264.0	561.2	167.5	129.3		134.6	24.6
1996/97	64.4	63.2	1013.3	95.1	650.8	1038.7	199.3	453.4	262.9	460.7	148.5	113.8	11.2[h]	205.1	24.0
1997/98	53.9	42.2	970.1	117.1	370.5	1212.7	125.9	482.3	331.8	440.6	191.0	116.7	21.3[h]	148.6	29.0
1998/99	96.8	77.5	999.5	136.6	860.8	1234.1	206.7	467.2	548.2	403.2	119.5	132.7	13.8[h]	169.6	28.6
1999/00	58.0	93.2	1024.5	89.1	865.2	1497.4	275.1	594.7	295.7	200.0	270.7	122.3	15.5[h]	175.0	33.5
2000/01	57.8	146.7	1017.2	102.7	386.6	1371.3	215.4	682.7	149.1	164.1	252.9	119.7	17.3[h]	176.2	29.8
2001/02	62.0	164.8	966.0	76.3	598.6	1612.3	216.3	710.3	504.7	160.9	217.1	111.9	17.2[h]	127.9	36.8
2002/03	60.8	156.9	1083.2	106.5	531.5	1635.0	229.2	561.0	611.9	156.7	205.9	124.7	16.7[h]	165.2	62.4
2003/04	67.8	174.8	980.4	101.0	727.0	1582.2[h]	290.7	622.1	458.7	203.6	215.6	111.6[f]	14.9[h]	130.2	69.9

a Surveys conducted in spring
b Number of breeding pairs
c Surveys conducted in December until 1998; in 1999 a January survey replaced the December count
d Surveys conducted in January
e Surveys conducted in fall through 1998; from 1999 to present a fall index is predicted from breeding ground surveys (total indicated pairs)
f Survey incomplete
g Only TGPP counted in Central Flyway range are included
h Indirect or preliminary estimate

Appendix K. Population indices (in thousands) for light goose, greater white-fronted goose, brant, emperor goose, and tundra swan populations during 1969-2004.

Year	Light geese				White-fronted geese		Brant		Emperor geese[a]	Tundra swans	
	Greater snow geese[a]	Mid-continent[b]	Western Central Flyway[c]	Western Arctic & Wrangel[d]	Mid-continent[d]	Pacific[e]	Atlantic[c]	Pacific[c,f]		Western[c]	Eastern[c]
1969/70	89.6	717.0						141.7		31.0	55.0
1970/71	123.3	1070.1					151.0	149.2		98.8	58.2
1971/72	134.8	1313.4					73.2	124.8		82.8	62.8
1972/73	143.0	1025.3	11.6				40.8	125.0		33.9	57.1
1973/74	165.0	1189.8	16.2				87.7	130.7		69.7	64.2
1974/75	153.8	1096.6	26.4				88.4	123.4		54.3	66.6
1975/76	165.6	1562.4	23.2				127.0	122.0		51.4	78.6
1976/77	160.0	1150.3	33.6				73.6	147.0		47.3	76.2
1977/78	192.6	1966.4	31.1				42.8	162.9		45.6	70.2
1978/79	170.1	1285.7	28.2	528.1		73.1	43.5	129.4		53.5	78.6
1979/80	180.0	1398.1	30.5	204.2		93.5	69.2	146.4		65.2	60.4
1980/81	170.8	1406.7	37.6	759.9		116.5	97.0	194.2	93.3	83.6	92.8
1981/82	163.0	1794.0	50.0	354.1		91.7	104.5	121.0	100.6	91.3	72.9
1982/83	185.0	1755.4	76.1	547.6		112.9	123.5	109.3	79.2	67.3	86.5
1983/84	225.4	1494.5	60.1	466.3		100.2	127.3	133.4	71.2	61.9	81.1
1984/85	260.0	1973.0	63.0	549.8		93.8	146.3	144.8	58.8	48.8	93.9
1985/86	303.5	1449.3	96.6	521.7		107.1	110.4	136.2	42.0	66.2	90.9
1986/87	255.0	1913.8	87.6	525.3		130.6	109.4	108.9	51.7	52.8	94.4
1987/88		1750.5	46.2			161.5	131.2	147.0	53.8	59.2	76.2
1988/89	363.2	1956.1	67.6	441.0		218.8	138.0	135.2	45.8	78.7	90.6
1989/90	368.3	1724.3	38.6	463.9		240.8	135.4	151.6	67.6	40.1	89.7
1990/91	352.6	2135.8	104.6	708.5		236.5	147.7	131.7	71.0	47.6	97.4
1991/92	448.1	2021.9	87.8	690.1		230.9	184.8	117.7	71.3	63.7	109.8
1992/93	498.4	1744.2	45.1	639.3	622.9	295.1	100.6	124.4	52.5	62.6[g]	76.6
1993/94	591.4	2200.8	84.9	569.2	676.3	324.8	157.2	130.0	57.3	79.4	84.5
1994/95	616.6	2725.1	146.4	478.2	727.3	277.5	148.2	133.7	51.2	52.9[g]	81.3
1995/96	669.1	2398.1	93.1	501.9	1129.4	344.1	105.9	126.9	80.3	98.1	79.0
1996/97	657.5	2850.9	127.2	366.3	742.5	319.0	129.1	157.9	57.1	122.5	86.1
1997/98	836.6	2977.2	103.5	416.4	622.2	413.1	138.0	138.4	39.7	70.5	96.6
1998/99	803.4	2575.7	236.4	354.3	1058.3	393.4	171.6	129.2	54.6	119.8	109.0
1999/00	813.9	2397.3	137.5	579.0	963.1	352.7	157.2	135.0	62.6	89.6	103.1
2000/01	837.4	2341.3	105.8	656.8	1067.6	438.9	145.3	124.7	84.4	87.3	98.2
2001/02	639.3	2696.1	99.9	448.1	712.3	359.7	181.6	136.7	58.7	58.7	103.8
2002/03	678.0	2435.0	105.9	596.9	637.2	422.0	164.5	106.5	71.2	102.7	108.2
2003/04	957.6[h]	2154.1[g]	135.3	587.8	528.2	374.9	129.6	119.2	47.4	83.0	95.0

[a] Surveys conducted in spring.
[b] Surveys conducted in December until 1997/98; surveys since 1998/99 were conducted in January.
[c] Surveys conducted in January.
[d] Surveys conducted in autumn.
[e] Surveys conducted in fall through 1998; from 1999 to present a fall index is predicted from breeding ground surveys (total indicated birds).
[f] Beginning in 1986, counts of brant in Alaska were included with remainder of Flyway.
[g] Survey was incomplete.
[h] Preliminary estimate.

53